East Cheshire Walks – from Peak to Plain 2nd Edition

Graham Beech

Sigma Leisure

First edition Copyright © 1985, Graham Beech
Reprinted 1986,1987
Second edition © 1988, Graham Beech
Reprinted 1989, 1990, 1991, 1994
All Rights Reserved

ISBN: 1 85058 112 6

Published by:

**Sigma Leisure, an Imprint of
Sigma Press,
1 South Oak Lane,
Wilmslow,
Cheshire SK9 6AR**

Cataloguing in Publication Data

Beech, Graham
    East. Cheshire Walks.
    1. Eastern Cheshire. Walkers' guides
    I. Title
    914.27'1

Illustrations by Linda Knight

Photographs by the author except where indicated

Cover Photograph: Kettleshulme from Charles Head

Acknowledgment

The maps within this book are based on those of the Ordnance Survey, and are reproduced by permission.

**Printed in Great Britain by
Manchester Free Press,**

Foreword

It is often the case that one looks to the remoter parts of Britain to provide opportunities for walking and enjoying the countryside, and yet there are usually opportunities to be found much closer to home. Certainly the east of Cheshire is ar area offering a wide variety of walks, from the easy going on the edge of the Cheshire Plain to the often more strenuous terrain of the Peak Park fringe. In addition we are extremely lucky in the large number of footpaths available to the walker.

All the signs are that leisure time is increasing for everybody and many people are making use of the rights of way network for their recreation. This will inevitably bring great pressure on the infrastructure which must be maintained by landowners and local authorities. Many of the paths, particularly to the east of Macclesfield and along the Bollin Valley are managed by Countryside Rangers. It is their job to ensure that the paths are kept open and easily used, but also to minimise conflicts between the farming community and walkers. It is easy to forget that farmers are trying to earn a living in increasingly difficult times and that problems of gates left open or dogs running loose near livestock reflect badly on all walkers. Great efforts have been made to improve the condition of paths under Ranger management and many new stiles and signposts have been erected. This work will continue and if you should meet a Ranger whilst out on a walk please do stop and talk to them, they are always willing to help or to hear of any footpath problems you may have experienced.

The publication of a new edition of East Cheshire Walks is particularly appropriate at present, following the recent statements of policy for the rest of the century by the Countryside Commission, who see the opening up of the rights of way network as one of the most important tasks. Certainly there are many people who are wary of venturing into the wider countryside for fear of trespassing or getting lost. This book will certainly make the countryside of East Cheshire more accessible and enjoyable to many people and I hope that it will also encourage many more people to explore the footpaths throughout the area.

I particularly welcome this book because it offers walks for all. You do not have to be an expert for there are several easy routes to try, whilst the more experienced walker will also find walks to suit their taste. Rights of way are an important part of our heritage, I am sure that this book will enable more people to enjoy that heritage and also promote understanding and co-operation between all groups working in, living in and enjoying the countryside.

David A. Kitching
Head Ranger, East Cheshire
Cheshire County Council
Countryside & Recreation Department.

Preface
– to the first edition

This book contains descriptions of over 150 miles of varied walks, ranging from easy strolls to fairly strenuous hill walking. They reflect the nature of the terrain in the East Cheshire area – roughly extending from the plains of Mobberley to the uplands around Kettleshulme. Hopefully, there is something for everybody here!

Country walking is a rapidly growing pastime, and is no longer the exclusive province of tweed-jacketed elderly gentlefolk. The East Cheshire branch of the Ramblers Association, to which I belong, now boasts a membership of around 300, and their regular walks attract people aged from eight to nearly 80 years of age.

To meet the demands caused by this growth of interest in walking, we obviously need to maintain the maximum possible free access to the countryside. The present footpath network is just about adequate for our needs, but all walkers should help in keeping the footpaths open and well used. It is all too easy for footpaths to be forgotten, then overgrown, and effectively lost for all time. We are all – walkers, landowners and local authorities – temporary custodians of a unique heritage. Hopefully, this book will help to preserve that heritage.

It is customary, in a preface, for an author to acknowledge the help that he has received during the preparation of his book. My particular thanks must firstly go to the Ramblers' Association for the many happy walks which provided the inspiration for this book. Naturally, any errors are mine and mine alone! Also, my thanks to the great majority of landowners who help to maintain our local footpath network.

A Note to the second edition

Minor changes have been made to the walks in the first edition, and six new walks are added, making a total of 31 walks, covering an extra 51 miles. The same philosophy as before has been applied – a mixture of shorter easy walks including the new path to Hare Hill Gardens, with more challenging hill-country walks. Both the north and south of Cheshire are now represented, with walks around Disley and Congleton respectively.

Eventually, I'll get around to a third edition. So, if you have a favourite walk, don't hesitate to tell me.

Graham Beech   December 1987

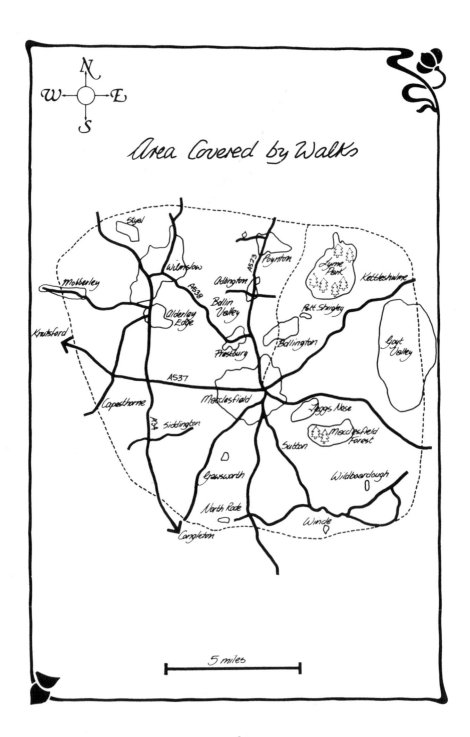

Area Covered by Walks

5 miles

CONTENTS

Introduction

This book came about as a result of my own walks in the Cheshire countryside. Although I have been interested in country walks for longer than I care to remember, it was only when I moved North to this area in 1980 and, a year later, joined the Ramblers' Association, that I really began to enjoy walking as a hobby. Another tangible benefit was that I learned more about the East Cheshire area in three months than I had in the previous twelve.

Walking is, of course, a rather strange hobby. It is, after all, something that we do for a large proportion of our waking lives and the majority of us seem to have mastered it fairly well. I haven't much in common with those experts who seek to make a cult about the esoteric aspects of walking, and I'm afraid the more extreme activities of back packing and long distance marathons don't attract me.

Whether with a group or on your own, walking provides the undeniable benefits of exercise, fresh air, and daylight. Walking with a group is also a social activity, whilst walking on your own, especially in little-known areas, is a challenge to your map reading and orientation skills.

But, enough of the philosophy; let's get down to basics and start enjoying the walks!

How to use this book

The book is divided into nine sections which deal with the following areas in alphabetical order:

Adlington, Poynton and Disley
Alderley Edge
Bollington
Gawsworth, Wincle and Congleton
Kettleshulme and Rainow
Prestbury
Siddington and The Peovers
Wildboarclough
Wilmslow and surrounding area.

Each walk contains a sketch map and detailed directions which should be sufficient to enable you to navigate your way successfully from start to finish. But, be warned: although the maps are *based* on Ordnance Survey maps, they are *not* intended as a replacement for them. I strongly recommend that you invest in one or more 1:25000 scale maps relevant to the area in which you intend to walk.

Each walk has a preliminary section, arranged in a standard format. The main points to remember are:

1. The *duration* is the time it takes me to complete the walk. For longer walks when darkness is likely to be a problem, please be sure that you can get back in time. Allow extra time if you are leading a group or if you are walking with children.

2. The *starting point* is given both as a description and as a grid reference, e.g. SJ849713. This is a unique identification which pinpoints any chosen location. For anybody unfamiliar with the notation, here is how it works:

   (i)   The first two letters identify the O.S. map. For example, the Macclesfield 1:25000 Pathfinder map is designated as SJ 87/97, because it was compiled from the original O.S. sheets SJ87 and SJ97.

   (ii) The first three digits are called the Eastings. Look at the horizontal numbering on the map until you find, in the Macclesfield example above, 84. Then count off nine of the ten smaller divisions between 84 and 85 – this gives you your East/West position.

   (iii) Similarly, the last three digits (the Northings) identify your North/South position. All you now have to do is to find the intersection of the two positions.

3. The walks are *graded* as follows:

   Easy: mostly flat with few difficult obstacles.

   Moderate: some hill climbing and/or difficult terrain.

   Strenuous: best avoided if you are accompanied by a young family!

Actually, I've yet to find a really strenuous walk in East Cheshire – it's gentle, rolling country with hill walks *just* tough enough to work up a thirst.

What do you need?

Apart from this book and, if possible an O.S. map – very little. Disregard those who want to load you up like a Victorian explorer – you're going to enjoy yourself. However, here's what I regard as a sensible minimum:

Waterproofs – any sort really, although the type that "breathes" is best. Rainfall in Cheshire is statistically no worse than anywhere else, but it always seems as though it is.

Boots – or any footwear with a discernible tread: some people use wellies for winter walks and trainers for the summer. I wear boots all the year round.

Rucksack – the smaller the better, within reason.

Compass – this takes the guesswork out of walking. Be sure to get the type with a flat perspex base and practise in the garden before using it for real!

Map – and learn how to read it.

Apart from the usual topographical symbols (for churches and the like), the most useful map feature to follow is a field boundary. Of course, many of these have been removed in the name of progress, but the ones that remain are invaluable because you can so easily relate the field that you are standing in to its outline on the map.

To this list you can add cameras, walking sticks, whistles and what-have-you. I prefer to keep life simple.

Rights of Way – and other countryside matters

The footpaths in this book are all public rights of way unless otherwise noted. A great number of paths are unsigned, either accidentally or deliberately, but they are still rights of way.

Please be sure that you do stick to the paths and do the things that any sensible person does, like shutting farm gates and generally respecting the country way of life. Surely, I don't have to tell anybody about the Country Code? When paths cross fields you may have a slight problem – if only just a struggle with your conscience: should you cross the field, possibly walking over a crop, or should you walk around the edge? Strictly speaking, if a public right of way exists you are within your rights to follow it unless a diversion has been granted. Where the maps in this book cross cultivated fields, it is because, at the time of writing, such diversions have either not been applied for or have been rejected.

These diversions are a sticking point between ramblers and land owners. Increasingly, more and more fields are being merged, with the loss of hedgerows.

Very often, footpaths used to follow the hedgerow so that we now have the prospect of the path crossing the new "superfield". Legally, if no diversion exists, a farmer must leave the footpath intact and uncultivated but, in practice, paths are often lost in this way.

I have no extreme views on the subject, though I prefer to see paths retained. I strongly object to making a half mile detour around a field, when the path used to be a 100 yard direct line. If you encounter problems with paths, first try discussing it with the landowner and then, if necessary, complain to the local council and/or pressure groups such as the Ramblers' Association. But, first and foremost – be sure of your facts!

On a somewhat related subject, an increasingly common problem is the grazing of bulls on land adjacent to public paths. Some say that most breeds are harmless and that bulls are quite docile when kept with heifers. I have not put either theory to the test and have always made an illegal detour to avoid a confrontation with a bull. Ironically, my brother-in-law and I were once chased by a herd of *cows* that, we kept telling ourselves, were just being playful!

Generally, you will find that the local farmers are happy to see you and fully respect your wish to share in the enjoyment of the countryside. I met a farmer near Bollington who was kindness itself, and very anxious to tell me about the area: he even welcomed the fact that I was going to lead a group of ramblers across his land a few days later!

There can, of course, be the other sort, and it is worth recounting the one experience which is almost the only time that I've had a hostile reception (it would be churlish to identify the gentleman concerned). As I was walking from the farm, he called out:

"Enjoying your walk?"
"Yes, thank you", said I, innocently.
"Oh no, you're not! You're just walking the paths."
"Well, I hadn't realised that there was a law against it. Actually, I'm writing a book of local walks – that's why I'm carrying a notebook."

This did not impress him. Seemingly, he felt that the planners had "done the dirty" on him by designating his farm track as a right of way. As we chatted, and the atmosphere became more friendly, it emerged that he had erected a "no entry – trespassers will be prosecuted" notice but those "council people" had made him take it down.

He was adamant that I should not follow my intended route, claiming that:

"When you get up there, you won't know where you are – so just go straight over the hill".

Well, I knew where I was going – and it wasn't over the hill! However, he relented and thought that my map and compass would probably save the day.

This sort of episode happens infrequently, thank goodness. Most of the time you'll receive a friendly greeting. If not, stand your ground and blame me!

A final point to remember: the descriptions of these walks are believed to be correct at the time of writing (1984 to 1987). But it is always possible that signs, stiles, trees and other landmarks may disappear and new ones appear in their place. May I, therefore, offer my apologies to any landowner whom I may have slighted in describing difficult access to a path – the problem could well be resolved by now!

Note – Thanks to my readers, a few small errors have been corrected from the first edition. With the passage of time, other changes may take place so I will look forward to readers' comments and suggestions in the event of there being a third edition.

Big Low – from Blaze Hill, on the outskirts of Bollington

Poynton Pool

Adlington, Poynton & Disley

Although geographically adjacent, these two areas provide an interesting contrast. Adlington is now almost entirely agricultural, while Poynton is a much larger settlement with many obvious clues to its industrial past.

The name Adlington is derived from Eadulvington – early Saxon for "the place or farm of Eadwulf's people". This is a good indicator to its agricultural origins. In the 19th Century some small-scale mining took place, but not on the scale of nearby Poynton. Rather more important was the quarrying of stone – particularly the valued "blue stone" from nearby Styperson, and brickmaking: several old brickyards are recorded on the O.S. maps and some derelict remains can still be found.

Poynton was originally part of the great sprawl of Prestbury, and only became a separate parish in 1871. It was very much the mining town of the area and, at one time, there were over fifty shafts spread over two miles. None of these was particularly deep – typically no more than 40 yards – but their output was significant enough for the Vernon family to make their fortunes. This was aided by the arrival of the canal in 1831 and the railway in 1845. Interestingly, both of these were good news for Poynton's coal industry, but the main impact of the railway on Adlington was to permit the rapid and inexpensive transport of milk, thus accelerating the return of Adlington to its agricultural base.

Whilst the Vernons were an important Poynton family, the Leghs of Adlington are rather more well-known locally. The family fortune again owes a lot to coal mining, though the Legh family can trace its Adlington ancestry back to the 14th Century. The most notable Legh connection is, of course, Adlington Hall. The Great Hall was built during 1450 to 1505, whilst the Elizabethan black and white addition was built in 1581. The gardens are quite beautiful, being the work of that amazing 18th Century artisan, Capability Brown; well worth a visit while you're in the area.

The hall and gardens of Lyme Park are, of course, better known. The park covers over 1300 acres in which are included a superb children's playground, a pitch and putt course and a large and well-established herd of deer. Although these attractions are known to most local people, it is surprising how few have visited the hall itself. This was the home of the Legh family, but was acquired by the National Trust in 1947. The interior is sparsely furnished, but is well worth seeing for its intricate pearwood carvings. Children always enjoy visiting the hall as there is a quiz for them to complete.

The Walks

It is part of the charm of walks in this area that they almost always combine lush agriculture with the industrial past, a stately home, or all three! The terrain varies from pancake-flat to moderately hilly – particularly as you stride through Lyme Park. From here, you also get tantalising glimpses of the real hills of the Pennine range lying to the East.

The walks range from six to twelve miles over moderately hilly ground. For a long, stimulating walk you should tackle walk APD3 which has a good blend of interesting features and some first-class scenery.

Adlington Hall (By permission, Cheshire Life)

Walk: APD1

Area: Adlington.

Starting Point: Lay-by on A523 near to the Legh Arms, Adlington (S J911804).

Route: Adlington, Adlington Basin, Styperson Pool, Adlington.

Length: Six and a half miles. Easy/Moderate.

Duration: About two and a half hours

This varied walk combines pleasant rambles through meadows and woods, a stroll along a canal tow-path and a visit to one of the few lakes in the area. Hopefully, this variety more than makes up for the almost unavoidable one mile stretch of road walking involved. Fortunately, the road is not a busy one, and if you feel really strongly about it, you can contrive a detour of about two miles or so.

Starting at the lay-by (1) on the A523 near the Legh Arms, turn left along Brookledge Lane then, after a few hundred yards, turn right into Wych Lane (2). This road peters out into a track, taking you past Wych Wood . 'Wych' rhymes with the first syllable of 'lychee', not with 'witch', so the locals tell me, though there are also tales about a witch who used to live in this wood. One thing that is certain, however, is that Wych Wood is one of the prettiest bluebell woods around, and is well worth a visit in late Springtime; there are numerous unofficial paths through the wood.

Staying with the main track, this eventually bends sharply to the right, at which point you go over a stile, and through a field to Harrop Green Farm (3).

About 100 yards after the farm, turn right at a stile adjacent to a gate and walk under the electricity cables, keeping the hedge immediately on your right until you are approximately half way across the field. At this point, turn left towards a stile near a large oak tree, to the right of a small wood.

You then cross the next field, heading slightly to the right of the top left corner. Here, three stiles (if you include the "gap" adjacent to the signpost) cross the old

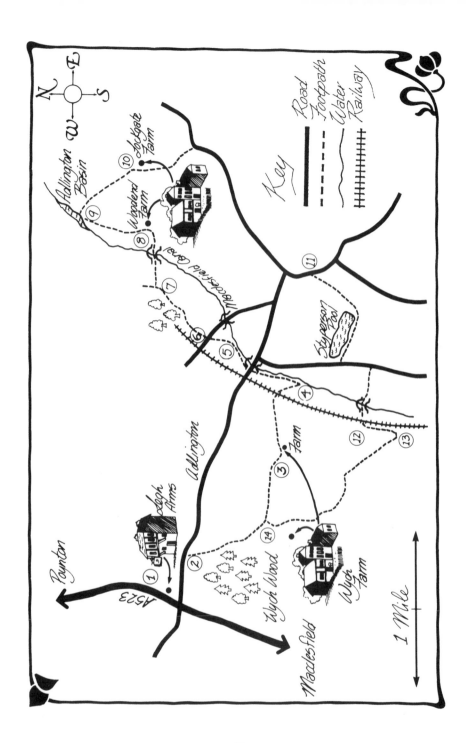

railway track, now a cycle track and footpath from Bollington to Poynton. The path in this next field is fairly obvious: it keeps to the right of a wood, and then leads to a bridge over the Macclesfield Canal. At the bridge, turn left, and join the tow path (4), keeping the canal on your right.

The tow path passes under a road bridge, and after a further 100 yards, you go through a stile (on your left – you'll get wet otherwise)(5) and cross a field diagonally, bearing right to another stile, to join a path where you again turn right towards a gate. At this point, cross the road to yet another stile on the left of the gate opposite you. Springbank Farm (6) is on your left and the signpost points to Jepson Clough.

Walk along a well-made track until you reach a hedge surrounding a small wood. Keeping the wood on your left, circle around it until you join a path which crosses a small bridge over a stream. Pass through the stile immediately after the bridge and head uphill to a stile about 50 yards to the left of Jepsonclough Farm (7).

Turn left here, onto a tarmac drive. After about 50 yards, take a right fork to another drive which passes first through a small wood, and then through a caravan site.

At the end of this drive, turn left just before Woodend Farm (8) to Adlington Basin (9). It's difficult to get lost on this stretch of the walk, so I'll leave it to you to find your way through the fields! The basin is a popular halt for pleasure craft and this is quite a good place for you to stop for a few minutes before beginning the uphill stretch of the walk.

At the basin, turn right along a track to Lockgate Farm (10). NOTE: this is NOT the first collection of buildings. The farm is at the very end of the track. Immediately beyond the farm, turn right at a stile, then on to a second stile, and cross a large field at an angle of 45 degrees towards the far hedge. After walking for a short distance with the hedge on your right, pass through a stile adjacent to a gate and proceed along a grass track to the main road. Turn right onto the main road, and have a rather boring time walking along it for almost a mile (actually, it's not too bad, and there's no easy alternative). Ignore the turn to Adlington; and very soon you will find a footpath sign (11) on the right, leading to Styperson Pool, which is rather more photogenic seen looking back from a few hundred yards further along the road.

A path leads down the hill and past the pool to a road, where you turn left towards Winterfold Farm. Before the farm, immediately before a cottage, turn right along a path which takes you back to the canal. Cross the canal, heading towards Higher Doles Farm (12), along a track which passes under the old railway line; if the ground in the tunnel is just *too* soggy, you can walk along the new footpath and join the correct one a couple of hundred yards further on – your exit is signposted "Holehouse Lane", then turn left along a rough track to a house called "Oakdene" (13).

From here, the directions need to be followed rather carefully.

Keep Oakdene on your right, and pass through a gate. Keeping the hedge on your right, go over a stile in the top right hand corner of the field then over a very small footbridge 40 yards inside the field. From here, head over to the right and, after about 100 yards, pass through a stile in the hedge and then through the next one facing you, in line with the house in front of you. Walk alongside the hedge, in front of the house; go through a gate and then straight ahead, under the electricity cables (again!). From here keep the hedge on your immediate right, and pass through the stile in the corner of the field.

Turn left at this stile, follow the hedge on your left and cross a small plank bridge to another stile (there is almost a record number of stiles on the particular walks in this book – one has a staggering 38) then turn right, following the hedge with Wych Farm on the far left.

Nearly home now: cross another stile and walk almost straight across the field, heading slightly to the left. This brings you onto a track (14) which leads left to Wych Farm. Turn right instead, then left and you're back at Wych Wood – which is almost where you started. Just keep walking back to Adlington.

Styperson Pool.

Walk APD2

Route: Poynton, Higher Poynton, part of Lyme Park

Starting Point: Car Park on South Park Drive, Poynton (off the A523 from Poynton to Hazel Grove). SJ922840

Length: Six miles. Moderate.

Duration: Two and a half hours, approximately.

The car park is just a few hundred yards along South Park Drive. In the event that this car park is full, try the alternative one in Anglesey Drive (point number 18 on the map) and start from there instead.

This walk takes you through part of the earlier coal mining area of Poynton, over an old railway line and the canal, each of which contributed to the area's previous mineral wealth. All of this is now, of course, long gone but the remains are still easy to find. If you want to explore the industrial archaeology of the area, one of the most useful publications is "Poynton's Pits" published by Macclesfield Groundwork Trust.

But now to our walk. Leave the South Park Drive car park (1) and turn left. At the T-junction, turn right and, after a short distance, cross the stile on your left (2).

The path now goes straight ahead, passing a large pool on your right. After about 50 yards, fork to the right along a path towards a copse. The path is really more of a track – being slightly elevated and running through a wood (3).

Cross the road (4) and then continue along Prince Road – a very minor byway. Then, cross Carleton Road and go over the bridge across the old railway which ran through this part of Poynton. This is now a cycleway and footpath (for those who enjoy man-made "organised" recreation), but was clearly important as a means of transporting coal and other commodities.

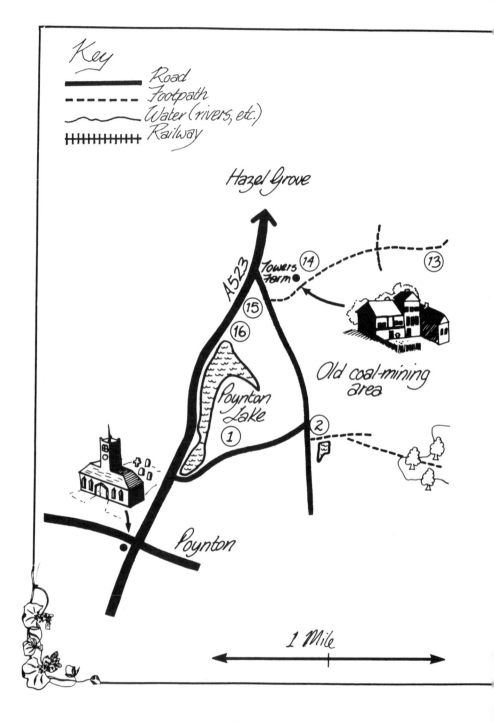

Key

Road
Footpath
Water (rivers, etc.)
Railway

Hazel Grove

A523

Towers Farm ●

⑭

⑬

⑮

⑯

Poynton Lake

①

②

Old coal-mining area

Poynton

1 Mile

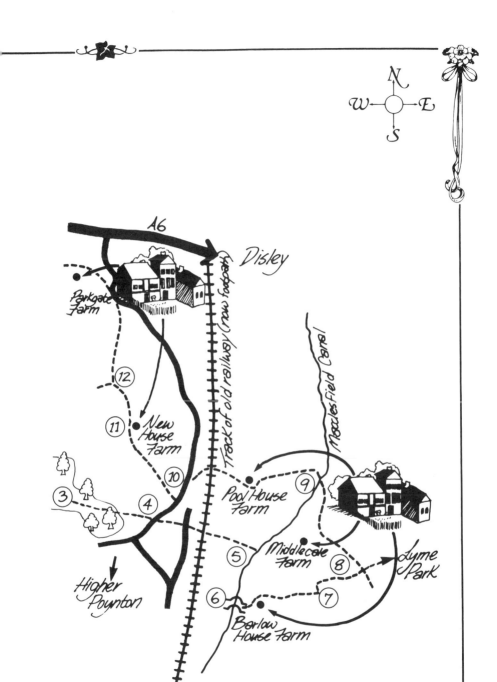

The path now continues towards the canal, just before which you will see quite extensive remains of buildings associated with the local mining activities. Turn right (5) at the canal and follow the towpath to a bridge (6), which you cross, leading you towards Barlow House Farm. The large PRIVATE sign does not, of course, apply to you – only to vehicles. Follow the path to the left of the farm. (Part of this is, in fact, a concessionary path but it is the best one to use.) The path runs the length of a field to the left of the farm's boundary fence. At the end of the field, still quite near to the farm, cross a stile adjacent to a gate and continue in the same direction that you were travelling. The Lyme Cage folly is now visible ahead and to your right.

At the end of the next field, go through a large wooden gate (7) and turn left. After 50 yards turn right over a stile and resume your previous direction of travel alongside a fence on your left.

Cross the next stile and turn left (8) to walk towards Middlecale Farm. Just before the farm, turn right and walk along the drive as far as the canal. Cross the canal bridge and immediately turn left along a track between a pair of hedges (9). At the end of this track, turn left over a stile and head for Pool House Farm. Cross the stile just before the farm, turn left and walk along the drive between the house and outbuildings. Then, follow the farm drive which crosses the old railway track to become a lane (Pool House Road).

At the end of this lane turn left and walk along the road until just before a telephone box. Turn right and cross the road to a track which leads past a now-inappropriately named New House Farm. After the farm, the track bends to the left then, after a further 50 yards, you turn right at a gate (12). Walk through two fields, with the hedge on your right. At the end of the second field, cross the stile into a wood. Now head downhill at about 45 degrees, heading towards a sharp bend in the road at the foot of the hill.

Walk along the road for a short distance and then turn left along the drive to Parkgate Farm. Go through the farmyard and head towards the wood. On leaving the wood, cross a stile adjacent to a gate (13) and follow the path to Towers Farm (14) – very prominent with its high silos. About 50 yards past this farm squeeze through a "stile" – actually a gap in the fence and head for a gate by the road (15). Cross its adjacent stile and turn right along the road, at the end of which notice the old Park Lodge.

Turn left at the A523; although the main road is painfully busy, you'll soon find a path set a little further back. Soon, you cross Anglesey Drive (16). Follow the path alongside the lake back to South Park Drive and your car.

Walk APD3

Route: Higher Poynton to Furness Vale, by way of Lyme Park and the Dipping Stone.

Starting Point: Lay-by opposite the Boar's Head, Higher Poynton.

Length: 12 miles. Moderate/strenuous.

Duration: Four and a half hours.

This fairly lengthy walk includes a good variety of attractions – an old railway track, a canal, reservoirs, a stately home (with a herd of deer) – and a curiosity in the shape of the Dipping Stone, more of which later.

From the lay-by(1), walk towards the Boar's Head, then turn right up the lane which passes over the old railway track. Opposite to a group of houses called "Mount Vernon", (presumably a reference to the old coal baron) join the canal towpath, turning right to head south (i.e. with the canal on your left).

Cross over the canal by the footbridge (2), noticing the remains of a swing-bridge that, presumably, preceded this bridge. The footpath leads diagonally to the right away from the bridge, passing Throstlenest Farm and then turning right in front of Green Farm (3).

From here, follow the farm drive until you reach the lodge for Lyme Park. Go through West Park Gate (4) and take the first right fork to cross the stream. Follow the left-most path up the hill, with the stream on your left to start with, passing through a small disused quarry and a plantation of rhododendrons. You should find this part of the route quite easily – it is well-walked. As the landscape opens up, you will see a ruined building (5) ahead of you. After reaching this, walk towards the wood that is facing you, keeping it on your left at first. After a short distance a path leads through the wood, heading gradually towards the wall on your right, where you should find a gate. Go through this, and follow the path around a pool; the path then broadens out and leads towards Lyme Hall. Notice the Lyme Cage folly beyond the hall – you may feel like a quick sprint up to it later. And, if you have not visited Lyme Hall, now is the time to do it.

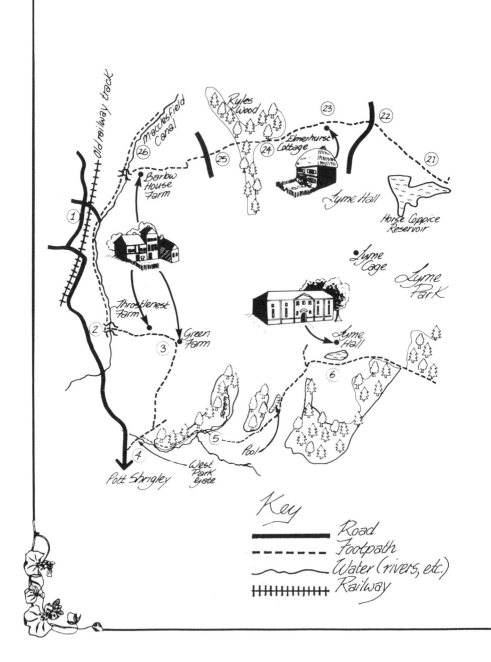

Old railway track

Macclesfield Canal

Ryles Wood

23

22

Elmerhurst Cottage

21

26

25

24

Lyme Hall

Barlow House Farm

Horse Coppice Reservoir

1

Lyme Cage

Lyme Park

Throstlenest Farm

2

3

Green Farm

Lyme Hall

6

5

Pool

4

West Park Gate

Pott Shrigley

Key

———— Road

- - - - Footpath

～～～ Water (rivers, etc.)

++++++++ Railway

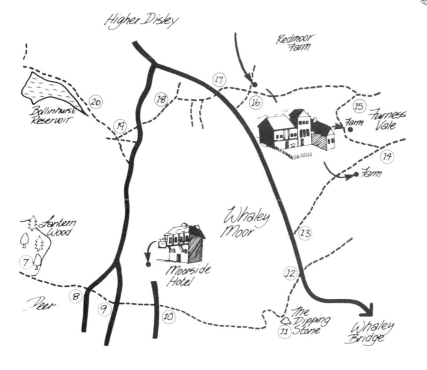

Higher Disley

Redmoor Farm

20 Ballinhurst Reservoir

18

17

16

19

15 Farm · Furness Vale

14 Farm

Lantern Wood

7

Whaley Moor

23

Moorside Hotel

12

Deer

8

9

10

11 The Dipping Stone

Whaley Bridge

1 Mile

The path that we require passes to the south side of Lyme Hall, in front of the lake (6). It is signposted "Gritstone Trail" and runs alongside the gardens of the hall. After passing the hall, the path then goes through the Deer Sanctuary (a good place to ask for if you get lost), keeping straight ahead with the fence on your right. After a while, the path crosses over a stream and leads to a gate. Cross the stile adjacent to the gate and walk with the wood on your right. You then pass a wall separating you from Lantern Wood (7).

After this wood, cross a stone stile and you will see the Moorside Hotel ahead of you. If you imagine a line drawn between you and the hotel, your path leads a few degrees to the right of this line and takes you to a minor road (8). Cross this and go over a stile and straight ahead. The path is to the right of a large house on your left. Continue straight ahead, with a stream about 50 yards to your left, until you cross another road (9).

Cross the road, to a stile facing you. Go over this, head downhill and to your left to cross another stile then a stream. The path now heads straight uphill – work your way around a large clump of gorse then walk uphill with a stream and fence on your right. Continue in this direction crossing a track (10), after which the path runs beside a wall on your right.

At the far end of the field, a ladder stile crosses the wall, and the path now becomes quite an obvious track, eventually crossing a further stile from where the outskirts of Whaley Bridge can be seen. Follow the obvious track from now on as it meanders across the moor. Eventually, you come to a high point from which you begin to drop down to a road, clearly visible in front of you. The Dipping Stone (11) is now on your right, so be sure to make a small diversion to inspect it, even though this requires a small trespass from your right of way. The origins of this stone – actually resembling an old kitchen sink – are obscure. Some say that it was used for cleansing coins in vinegar or some similar substance to avoid passing infection between parishes, but I've yet to verify this.

Now, return to the main path and continue to the road; where you turn left (12). Walk along the road (ignoring the first stile on your right), until you reach a gate on the right hand side (13) leading towards a farm; a white-painted farm a little further ahead is also a good direction finder. Please note that the path you require is to the *left* of a wall and goes along an obvious track – judging from the "no footpath" signs around here, I suspect that the farmer has some problems with the rambling fraternity!

Go along this path to the farm, passing through the farmyard gate and between the two main farm buildings, then along a cobbled track.

The path passes a small reservoir and then, after a couple of hundred yards joins another farm track. Turn left here (14) and head towards the next farm, this being the white-painted house seen as you left the road.

The path runs to the left of the farm buildings, along the farm track, and leaves the farmyard through a gate. Be assured that this *is* a public right of way, whatever you may hear to the contrary.

Now, follow the track up the hill until you reach a ruined barn (15). Turn left at a stile adjacent to the gate facing the barn. The path goes into the field and is parallel with the wall 50 yards or so on the right.

Halfway across this field, turn left by 45 degrees and head for the stile facing you in the opposite wall.

Continue in the same direction to a stile adjacent to a gateway. The path now runs to the left of a fence, then a stone wall, towards Redmoor Farm (16).

Cross the farm drive and then go over a stone stile. The path leads to the right of the stone wall facing you and towards the road (the footpath sign is clearly visible).

Cross the road (17) to a stile; go over this and continue straight ahead to a stile near a prefabricated building. The path runs to the left of the wall from her, crossing another stile at the end of the field.

Cross the next field to a stile in the top right hand corner. Ahead of you are the reservoirs alongside which we will soon be walking.

From this stile, head towards the junction of two walls (18) ahead of you. Keep just to the left of the junction, carry on over a stile and head towards the road. Cross the road and join the next path, signposted "Lyme Park", go straight ahead towards the wood. After a short distance, you reach a stile near a track and a signpost to Kettleshulme. *Do not* follow this sign. Instead, turn right (do *not* cross the stile) and follow the path to the left of a stream with wooded banks. The path crosses the stream (20), leading to the easterly end of Bollinhurst Reservoir. Now follow the wall past this reservoir, then alongside the Water Board access track towards a farm (21). Go through the farmyard and cross the field facing you towards the stile adjacent to a gate, leading to a well-surfaced track.

This leads back towards Lyme Park. Turn left at the park gate and cross the main park drive (22). Go over a bridge, passing one cottage on your right and a second on your left. At Elmerhurst Cottage (23), follow the sign for Middlecale Woods and Middlewood.

The path eventually leads into a wood (24), over a stream and up a hill. You cross a stile to leave the wood and continue straight ahead. This path crosses the drive (25) to Middlecale Farm and enters a field with a hedge on your right.

Keep the hedge on your right and continue straight ahead until you reach a stile. Turn left and, after about 50 yards, turn right through a gate. The path now leads to the canal, past Barlow House Farm (26). Be sure not to cross their boundary fence or hedge – to help you, there are (or were) some waymarks, but the path is easy to follow. The path then joins a well-surfaced track and heads towards a bridge over the canal. After crossing this, turn left and walk along the towpath. Finally, turn right at the next bridge and you're back at the Boar's Head.

Deer in Lyme Park

Walk: APD4

Route: Disley, Mellor Moor and Strines.

Starting Point: car park behind Library at Disley

Length: 7½ miles. Moderate

Duration: 3½ hours

Start point: Disley Library car park SJ 9751847.

This is a brisk walk with fabulous views; its claim to fame in this book is that it is the most northerly walk; it also is unusual in passing through two golf courses!

Leave the car park and cross the main road (A6) to Jackson's Edge Road (1). Turn right at Stanley Hall Lane (2), signposted to Disley Golf Club. Already, you have excellent views of Mellor Moor on your right and, further away, Kinder Scout. I reckon this is the best way to see Kinder Scout – from as far away as possible! Fork left before the clubhouse along the drive past Stanley Hall. At a wood, the path bends sharply left; shortly after, turn right (3) by a group of silver birches to another small wood. Leave the wood by a stile and continue along a track to a minor road. The chimney on your left (4) is an old bone mill; its flue went down to the mill in the small valley below – all to get a good draught!

The track develops into a minor road, which brings you to a more major road (5), called The Ridge. Turn right here and, shortly after the Romper Inn, turn right again and head towards the canal. Cross the bridge and continue to the main road (6). Cross straight over and follow the River Goyt to a bridge; cross this, turn left and then fork right up a flight of stone steps. Follow the track to a viaduct over the railway. Cross this and continue straight ahead, through a gate, into our second golf course of the day (7); ignore the sign to Mellor, pointing left.

Follow the path through the golf course, passing a wood on your right. Turn left at the end of the wood (signposted for the 13th tee!) to a tarmac road, where you turn right (8) up hill. Turn right at the car park (9) just before a road and a group of houses. From here, follow the track past a house on your left to a junction of two paths (10). At the junction, turn left, along a sunken path between stone walls. This takes you to the edge of Mellor Moor (11), where you can stop to admire the view.

Turn right at a minor road – notice the large cross on your left, which was erected as a local community project! From here, it is – as they say – all down hill. Turn right at a gate, a short way after some houses; superb views of Kinder Scout are obtained from here (12).

Go down a grassy track; keep left along what turns into a loose stone track, then go straight ahead into a field, with a wall on your left. Cross two stiles; after the second, turn right to go to a minor road, where you turn left into the charming hamlet of Brook Bottom (13). Shortly after the Fox Inn, turn right along a path which takes you to the village of Strines; your route now continues along a road, passing a remarkable dove cote standing in the middle of a lake (14) – an inheritance of 19th century altruism! Cross the main road (15) and follow a track to the canal, where you turn left (16).

Continue along the canal until you reach a swing bridge (17), just after a house on your right. Cross the canal here, bear left and follow the track which eventually becomes Hagg Bank Lane, leading directly back to Disley. A tea shop and several pubs are available!

Fountain Square, Disley

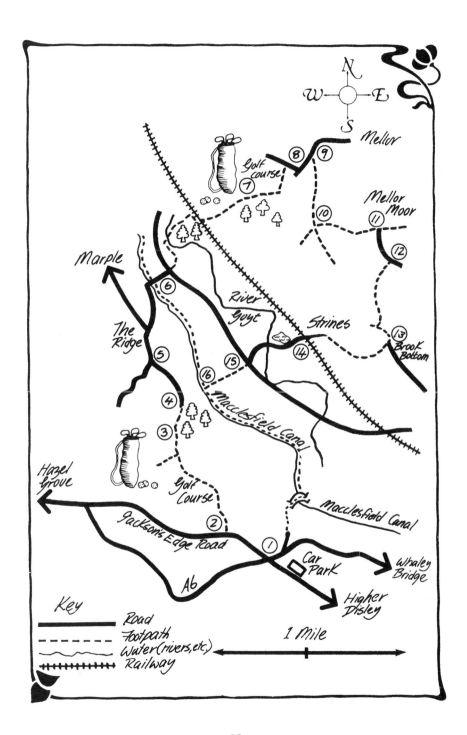

N
W E
S

Mellor

Golf course

⑧ ⑨

⑦

Mellor Moor

⑩

⑪

⑫

Marple

River Goyt

Strines

⑬ Brook Bottom

The Ridge

⑥

⑤

⑮

⑭

⑯

④

③

Macclesfield Canal

Hazel Grove

Golf Course

② Jacksons Edge Road

Macclesfield Canal

① Car Park

Whaley Bridge

A6

Higher Disley

Key

Road
Footpath
Water (rivers, etc.)
Railway

1 Mile

33

Alderley Edge

This area has three distinct facets:

- the village itself, now facing an identity crisis as Wilmslow continues to act as the focus for shoppers and business people.

- the residential area; like Wilmslow, many large houses were built in the mid-19th Century when the railway company offered a "perk" of a first class season ticket to and from Manchester for 20 years to anybody who built a house worth between £50 and £150.

- the surrounding countryside, based mainly on the Edge itself, on the way from the village of Alderley Edge to Macclesfield.

The Edge is owned by the National Trust, and this is the focus of the walks in this section. It draws visitors like a magnet, and a Sunday afternoon is definitely not the place to be if you fancy a quiet stroll. Indeed, the volume of visitors is so high that soil erosion is quite a problem.

But, whenever you do visit Alderley Edge, be sure to call at the Visitor's Centre, which is near to the main car park. This is open from Easter to October and will give you an immediate insight into the geography and history of the area.

As most local people will know, there are two things you ought to know about: the old mining industry, which is factual, and the legend of Merlin, which is entertaining but probably the product of a fertile imagination.

The two are linked, as you will shortly see. The legend claims that a farmer from nearby Mobberley met an old wizard-like man at Alderley Edge, whilst travelling to Macclesfield fair to sell his white horse. The old man offered to buy the horse, but the farmer refused causing the "wizard" to tell him that he would fail to sell the horse at the fair. When, later that day, the farmer returned with the unsold horse, our wizard character is said to have led him across The Edge, past Stormy Point to a rock which he tapped with his wand. Suddenly, a pair of iron gates were exposed, which opened into a cavern. Both of them – and the white horse – entered to see several more similar horses and their owners, all in a state of suspended animation and waiting for just one more horse to complete the "army" which would be able to suppress some ill-defined uprising. The farmer was allowed to help himself from a pile of gold and then to leave – he being luckier than the rest. If you have a taste for this sort of thing, I suggest that you might like to dip into "Legends and Traditions of Cheshire" by Frederick Wood, published by Shiva in 1982.

The link with reality is, of course, the mining activities in the area. The caves are mostly man-made and date back to 1708 when a small but unsuccessful mine was begun by a Mr. Abbadine, from Shropshire. Several other speculative mines were dug, but few of them were commercially successful. Copper ore was the main product of these mines, and the largest were Engine Vein – not far from the car park – and West Mine on the other side of the road. There have been attempts to open the larger caverns to the public, but these have failed to date. You can, however, visit some of the mines by arrangement with the Derbyshire Caving Club for a nominal fee.

The Walks

Our walks all begin at the main National Trust car park. Because The Edge is perched so high above the surrounding plain the beginning and end of any walk in this area has a modest amount of hill climbing. The two main walks in this section give you a fair contrast between the two sides of The Edge – one leading in the general direction of Mottram's fertile Cheshire farmland, and the other towards Nether Alderley with its contrasting history.

A View from The Edge

Walk: AE1

Route: The Edge and The Hough.

tarting Point: National Trust Car Park, Alderley Edge. (SJ860773)

Length: Three miles. Moderate.

Duration: One and a half hours.

Walk from the car park to the Information Centre, where you turn right and walk a short way along the private National Trust road. Turn left before the bungalow and walk along a well-made track (1). After a hundred yards or so, you enter a clearing. Go straight across this to a path which heads to the left. Cross over an intersection with the next path. In front of you, you will see a stone wall and, ahead to the right, an elevated mound supporting the remains of the Armada Beacon (2). The building which used to stand here was allowed to fall into disrepair and in 1931 was destroyed in a gale.

Whilst standing by the Beacon, turn so that you have your back to the stone wall and walk along the path facing you. Eventually, this path plunges downhill but you can make a short diversion to your right just before going downhill, to an open rocky viewpoint. This gives views extending from Woodford Aerodrome and the Welsh hills on your left to the Peak District on your right. As an added bonus, there are some small caves here for children to explore, with greenish copper-coated sandstone as evidence of the small scale mining that took place here. *Please* take great care if you do explore this area.

Return to the main path and carry on straight ahead, over a small rise. Do NOT head to the right and do NOT follow the bridlepath signs.

After the rise, the path continues downhill, veering slightly to the left. Where the path meets a field, turn left and follow the path down to the road (3). Cross the road to join the drive to Saddlebole Farm (believed to be a Bronze Age site of copper smelting: "bole" is the old English word for hearth). Turn left over a stile at the end of the drive and walk along the edge of the field, with the hedge on your right. At the end of the hedge, turn right and follow the next hedge as far as the road (4) where you turn right.

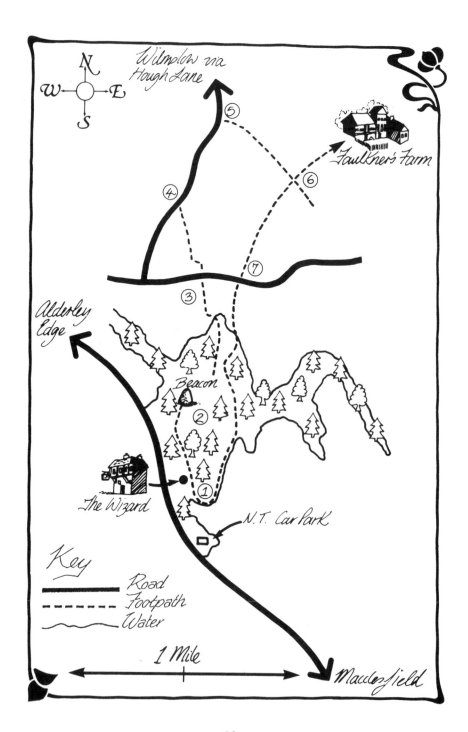

Wilmslow via
Hough Lane

N
W E
S

⑤

④

Faulkner's Farm

⑥

③

⑦

Alderley
Edge

Beacon

②

①

The Wizard

N.T. Car Park

Key

———————— Road
- - - - - - - - Footpath
∼∼∼∼∼∼∼ Water

1 Mile

Macclesfield

After a few hundred yards, turn right at the footpath opposite Brook Farm (5). Walk straight ahead – the path runs alongside the hedge after a hundred yards or so.

Immediately after a pool on your left, cross the stile and turn right. Turn right again at the next stile (6). NOTE: a little used path turns left here to Faulkner's Farm – this makes an excellent extension to the walk. Consult your O.S. map; you can easily follow this path, swinging round through Mottram Hall and back through Mottram St. Andrew.

But, for now, follow the path I suggested and continue with the hedge on your right. Cross a footbridge over Whitehall Brook.

According to the O.S. map, the path now goes straight across the field, but you might like to be kind to the farmer and walk around the edge keeping the hedge on your left, to a stile in the top-left corner.

Follow the hedge (on your left), go over two more stiles and you will meet the road to the left of Dickens Farm (7). Note that the farmhouse to your left sells drinks at the time of writing – this might be handy to know if you have children in tow.

Now, cross the road and follow whatever paths you like to the top of the Edge. You should easily be able to find your car. You really can't get lost here – when you get to the top of the Edge, turn left and be sure not to go downhill again. If the worst comes to the worst and panic sets in, there are invariably plenty of people to ask (except, of course, when you need them!).

Walk: AE2

Route: The Edge to Nether Alderley.

Starting Point: National Trust Car Park, Alderley Edge. (SJ860773)

Length: Six miles. Moderate.

Duration: Two and a quarter hours.

This walk is not quite so popular, though still well walked and signposted, so you won't lose your way. It includes Nether Alderley Church (St. Mary's) and Nether Alderley Mill, to make for a surprisingly varied walk.

Turn left out of the National Trust car park (i.e. along the main road towards Macclesfield) and take the first turn right along a minor road. Follow this road around a left hand bend and carry on as far as a sharp left hand bend (1). Here, you cross a stile and head for the opposite corner of the field. The path proceeds through two stiles and runs to the left of a hedge, then a fence. The path is clearly well used and passes through pleasant undulating pasture.

Where the path meets a road (2), turn right and go as far as a sharp left hand bend (3). Carry straight on, slightly to the right and follow the track signposted to Jarman's Farm.

Mid-way along the track between Jarman's Farm and High Park Farm, turn right at a stile (4) and follow first the fence and then a hedge as far as a tree stump (5) above a hedge to your right. Turn left here and head towards a large gap in the hedge slightly to your right. (In other words, you have turned left through an angle of about 70 degrees).

Go over the stile facing you and continue through the fields. You pass over a second stile then, when you get to the end of the next field (a gate should be facing you), turn right (6).

Cross the next stile and go through the next field, going through a large gap in the fence (you may now, find a gate, or the fence may have been completely removed). The path bends to the left, running beside a small wood, and through a stile.

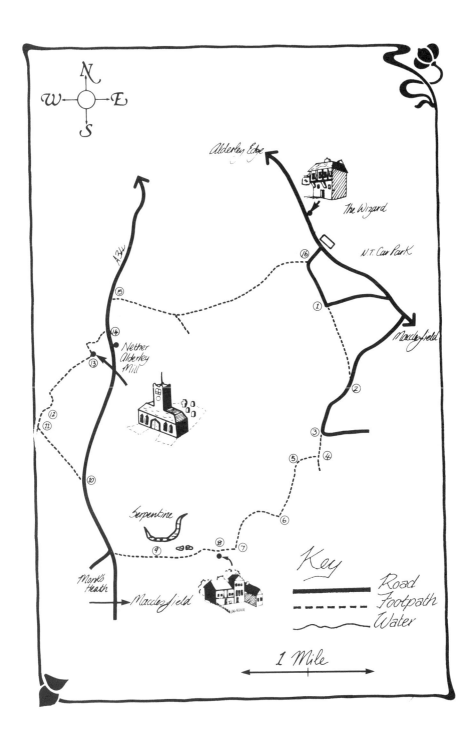

N W E S

Alderley Edge

The Wizard

N.T. Car Park

A34

(16)

(15)

(14)
(13)

Nether
Alderley
Mill

(1)

Macclesfield

(2)

(12)
(11)

(3)

(5) (4)

(10)

(6)

Serpentine

(8)
(9) (7)

Monks
Heath

Macclesfield

Key

Road
Footpath
Water

1 Mile

From here, the path lies straight ahead, over a small hill to the wood facing you. Your next stile is on the right, about 100 yards before the top right hand corner of the field (7). Cross this stile, another one after just a few yards and carry straight on.

Cross the stile to the right of the farm buildings (8) – you may care to observe the ICI complex on your extreme right. The path continues straight ahead and over a stile. There are some small pools on your right, and further to the right is "The Serpentine" (9) a meandering lake.

From this point (by the pools), the path follows the edge of the field, as far as a stile by an oak tree.

From here, head slightly left, passing two large cedars. The stile is about 30 yards to the left of where a stone wall ends. Cross the stile and you'll reach the A34 where you turn right. Note that there is a cafe at Matthews Nurseries, which might come in handy.

This stretch of road is unavoidable but do watch out if you have children with you. Carry on for about half a mile, then turn left (10) at the footpath sign (just after the "road bends" sign).

The path continues straight ahead, through a wood and over a stile. Continue over this stile straight towards the next stile and then – careful! – the next stile is a little to your left, entering a small wood.

When you emerge from the wood (11) turn right along a track past Heawood House (12). Carry on along the drive and follow the path to the right of the large house facing you. At the time of writing (November 1984) this was a "courtesy path" and an Order had been submitted to divert the previous right of way (currently going through a garden) along this new path. There is no inconvenience – so why object?

After the diversion keep straight ahead and follow the path to Nether Alderley Church (13), dating back to the late 14th Century and having particular associations with the Stanley family. It is a fascinating old church, and possesses many unusual items, including an 18th Century "Vinegar Bible". The origin of this name is interesting, but I'll let you find it out. If you do visit the church, a path runs from it to the A34, where you turn left. Alternatively, turn left at the wall surrounding the churchyard, where you originally arrived at the church, pass through a stile and over a stream. From here, turn right, follow the stream then turn left at the fence and follow it to the A34.

The stream that you walked alongside is the mill stream from Nether Alderley Mill – a working water powered mill now owned by the National Trust. After many years it was lovingly restored by a mill enthusiast and you really ought to visit it. So, turn right here (14) and the mill is on the opposite side of the road.

From the mill, head North towards Alderley Edge, again along the A34. After a quarter of a mile, turn right along Bradford Lane (15). After about half a mile, fork left and continue until you meet the road. Turn left here (16), then left at the main road, and you're back at the car park.

Nether Alderley Mill

<table>
<tbody>
<tr><td>

Walk: AE3

Route: The Edge and Over Alderley.

Starting Point: National Trust Car Park, Alderley Edge. (SJ860773)

Length: Four miles. Moderate.

Duration: One and a half hours.

</td></tr>
</tbody>
</table>

This walk covers some of the same ground as walk AE2, but it is substantially shorter and ideal for a summer evening.

Follow the directions for walk AE2 as far as the end of Slade Lane (3). Turn left and, after about 200 yards, turn right (4) at a stile signposted "Wrigley Lane". Go straight ahead, over two footbridges, then at the next stile (5), keep left and follow the fence until you meet the road, where you turn right.

About 200 yards before St. Catherine's church, with its unusual octagonal tower, turn right along a drive opposite to a cottage. Keep going straight ahead, through the farm – do not fork right – until you reach the next farm drive (7), where you turn left.

Follow the drive until you reach Bradford Lane (8), the cobbled lane that began at point (15) on map AE2. Turn right and follow the lane back to the road (9), where you turn left, then left again to arrive back at the National Trust car park.

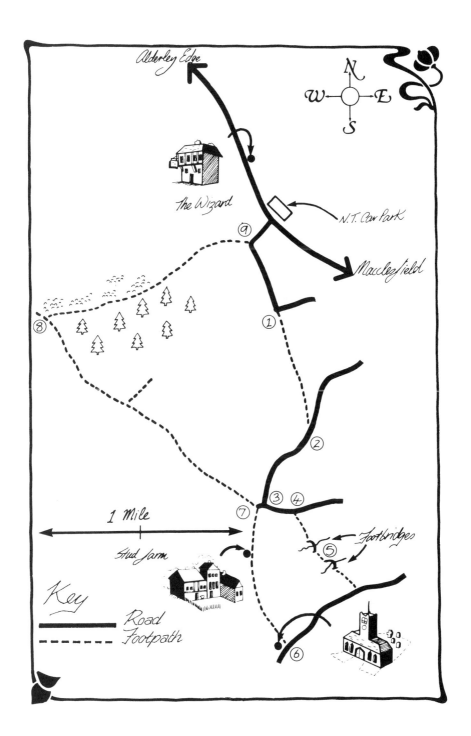

Alderley Edge

N
W E
S

The Wizard

N.T. Car Park

⑨

Macclesfield

⑧

①

②

③ ④

⑦

Footbridges

⑤

1 Mile

Stud Farm

Key

Road
Footpath

⑥

Walk: AE4

Route: Alderley Edge, Hare Hill and Bradford Lane

Starting Point: National Trust Car Park, Alderley Edge (SJ860773)

Length: 4½ miles. Easy

Duration: 2 hours

This is an easy stroll using a relatively new permissive path opened by the National Trust, which runs from Alderley Edge to Hare Hill. The best time to do the walk is in Spring time, so that you can visit the gardens at Hare Hill; these are famous for their azaleas and rhododendrons.

From the main car park (1), turn right along the track towards the Edge. Head to Edge House Farm, between two parallel wire fences. Cross over a stile at the farm and head downhill to the site just before Waterfall Wood. After the stile, our main route goes to the right, but, since access to the waterfall has been improved over the years, it's worth the small diversion to your left. The fall is unspectacular, but pretty.

Having turned right over the stile (with or without the waterfall excursion) continue alongside the field boundary, then turn left to Hill Top Farm (2). At the end of the farm drive, turn left beyond the farm itself, then right and up a flight of man-made steps signposted "Hare Hill" into Daniel Wood.

The walk through the wood is extremely pleasant — it's so nice to see some mixed woodland rather than the ubiquitous curse of the conifer. The path emerges from the wood and crosses to a gate, entering Alder Wood. Follow the path through this wood and then — following the way marks — continue to the lake (3), which is now a popular spot for a picnic. The way marks continue, taking you to Hare Hill gardens (4) which you really must visit (there is a small admission charge). Cross the car park and turn right along the main drive from the gardens to a minor road. Turn right here, and continue to the main Alderley-Macclesfield road. After 100 yards, turn left into Finlow Wood, then right onto a minor road. Where this road bends sharply to the right (6), carry straight on along a track to Finlow Hill Farm.

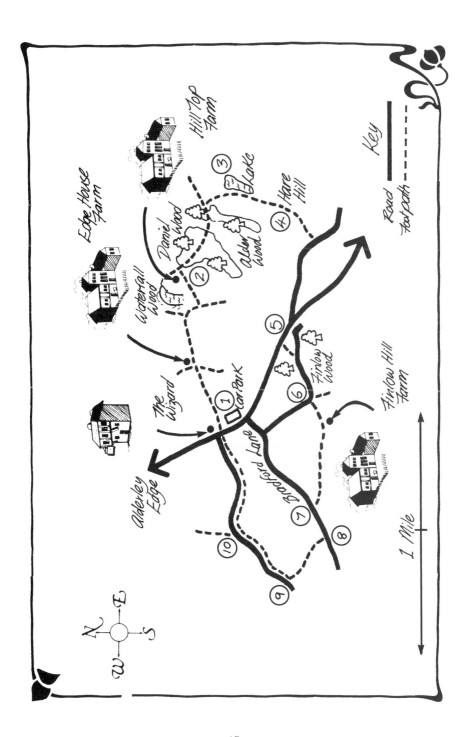

Go right over a stile before the farm, then carry on in the direction you were walking. At a fence, fork right and follow the path alongside a wood to a stile. This leads across a field to another stile, at Bradford Lane (7). Turn left here.

Walk along the lane for a while, then turn right at a stile just past a bungalow on your right (8). Follow the path, with the hedge on your right, to another stile; cross this, then keep the hedge on your left until you reach a minor road (9), where you turn right.

Carry on uphill. It is possible to lengthen the walk by using the path at (10), but it is perfectly pleasant to use the path alongside the road, which leads back to the Wizard and the car park.

A 'Kissing Gate' near Hare Hill Gardens

Bollington

The first thing that strikes a visitor about Bollington is its length – some 2.4 miles to be exact. After that, you notice the mills, a somewhat amazing number of public houses and even more small shops. The whole atmosphere is more typical of a small town in Ireland rather than a Cheshire village.

Bollington has its roots in silk and textiles. There is still some activity in this industry, such as Shrigley Dyers, but many of the mills have been deserted and Bollington now looks as though it has seen better days although, on the plus side, it has an above-average community spirit and is now having quite a revival as the numerous small properties are modernised. To get the feel of the area, a good booklet to read is "Bollington: Drift or Design" by Harry Ward (published for the 1974 Bollington Festival by Macclesfield Press Ltd.).

There are two particularly distinctive features to Bollington. One is the Macclesfield Canal aqueduct which spans the main street, and the other is "White Nancy", a monument at the end of Kerridge hill which can be seen from miles around. For such a popular monument, hard facts about it are difficult to come by. It now seems fairly certain that it was erected to commemorate the victory at Waterloo and was originally an open shelter – since bricked up due to vandalism and decay. The origin of its name is difficult to track down, but the most likely explanation is that it refers to the horse used to haul the construction materials up the hill!

The Walks

Due to the excellent hilly terrain, most of the walks in this section fall into the moderate/strenuous category. Anybody wanting to do some 'real' walking should start here!

Another publication that could be of interest is "Walks Around Bollington" – a pack of booklets prepared for the 1980 Bollington Festival. These are available from Bollington library.

Walk: B1

Starting Point: Turner's Arms, Bollington (SJ940779).

Route: Ingersley Vale, Rainow and Swanscoe Hall.

Length: Six miles. Moderate.

Duration: Approximately two hours.

Start at the Turner's Arms(1) in Ingersley Road. Walk along this road then, at the Poachers Inn, turn right down Mill Lane(2). At the end of Mill Lane, (bowling green on right) turn left, and pass the small row of cottages.

Immediately at the end of the cottages turn left and, just at the back of the last cottage, are steps and a stile (3) leading into a field. The path goes uphill and bears right, bringing you up to a wall on your left.

Look out for steps and a stile in the wall. Go through the stile (4), turn right and, after about thirty yards, turn left onto the barely-discernible track leading away from the factory in the valley and uphill towards the drive to Ingersley Hall Farm.

Cross over the main drive. Continue straight on towards a small wood (keep it on your left). This path goes through a stile adjacent to a wooden gate that then joins a road, at which point (5) you turn immediately right through a stile and walk towards Ingersley Hall Farm, keeping the wall on your right. Parts of this path have stone steps and paving – going back to the time when they were used as paths for mill workers. Unfortunately, parts are now missing so it can be muddy!

Carry on through two more stiles and you will then find a third stile on your right. Cross this and then continue walking on the right of the wall. Do not walk downhill at this point. On your right, as you pass through this field, you will see the White Nancy monument at one end of Kerridge Hill.

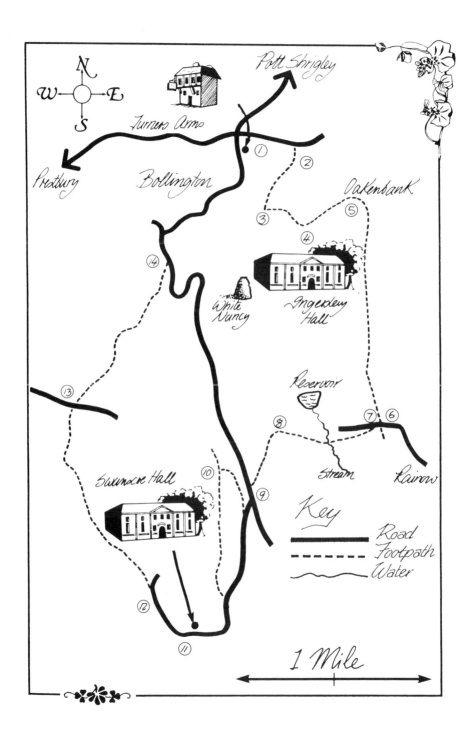

Continue walking to the end of the field. Go over the stile in the left hand corner and walk straight ahead to the next stile, again in the top left hand corner. After entering this field, walk across to a stile which is half way along the opposite wall. The stile in the next field is in the top right hand corner. Go through this and turn left towards Rainow, passing through two more stiles followed by a flight of stone steps and another stile, shortly after which you reach a minor road. Turn right here (6).

After a hundred yards, turn left up some steps (7) and into a field, keeping to the right. Cross two stiles towards a stream, at which point turn left and head uphill, past some old stone steps directly opposite the bridge. Your path leads very slightly to the right, heading for a gap in the trees at the top of the hill (8).

Carry on over the top to a wall, where you turn left. You should see the Sutton Common radio beacon on the skyline. Follow the path down to a road junction (9) and take the right fork facing you. Walk along this road to a farm drive on the right.

Now follow a long zig-zag, down to Swanscoe farm (10) where we turn left to head back along the valley. Go through a gate, then a stile and keep Lower Swanscoe Farm on your right. You now join a farm track, taking you towards a main road, where you turn right. Walk past the entrance to Swanscoe Hall (11), keeping to the road on the right. After a couple of hundred yards, again bear right, down a road signed as a "dead end".

Along this road, you enter a private drive (12) and after a few hundred yards, fork right. Follow this path through two gates and walk past a barn on your left, then a small pool by a gate. Walk through the gate, pass to the left of another pool, and cross the next field by walking between two pools to the opposite stile. There should be a white house facing you. Cross the field to a stile adjacent to a gate, and follow the path to the right of the white house. This continues over a road (13) where a small bridge crosses a stream – keep left after this and walk to the left of a hedge. (On your far left is the canal and in front is the old Adelphi cotton mill).

There is now a pleasant stroll through a succession of small fields all well provided with stiles. The path finally joins a road (14) opposite Holy Trinity Church at Kerridge.

Turn left here, walk along the road and turn right into Chancery Lane. Then, along Lord Street, Church Street, and back to the Turner's Arms.

Note: As a variation, also making for a slightly shorter walk, turn right when you reach the top of Kerridge and walk along the ridge to White Nancy. On your right, you have a particularly impressive view of your route. From White Nancy, drop straight down the hill to Chancery Lane.

Walk: B2

Route: Bollington to Bowstones

Starting Point: Ingersley Road, Bollington (near Poachers Arms) SJ943779

Length: Ten miles. Strenuous.

Duration: Four and a half hours.

The walk to Bowstones is a popular one for keen walkers. The suggested route to Bowstones is mainly based on moderately well-surfaced tracks, thus giving you a fairly mud-free walk; unfortunately, the same cannot be guaranteed for the return excursion! Apart from seeing the Bowstones, a fair portion of Lyme Park is included in this exhilarating walk.

The suggested starting point has been chosen for ease of parking; the road from The Poachers Arms to The Country Cafe or The Cheshire Hunt is less suitable for parking, but having a meal at either establishment might provide you with free parking for the day!

From The Poachers Arms, walk up the hill, past Sowcar Cottage.

Turn left at the fork in the road (1), signposted to Pott Shrigley. After a short distance, there is a stile above a stone wall. Go through this stile, walk behind the Country Cafe and head towards the Cheshire Hunt Inn (2). Turn right at the gate and continue uphill along the road, ignoring the "Bowstones" footpath sign on your left – you will return by that route. Our route passes mainly to the south of Berristall Dale, with Andrew's Knob on the left as you walk along the road.

Eventually, the road leads downhill and past a house, terminating at a gate. Go through the stile, down the path and over Mellow Brook (3), which joins Harrop Brook on your left.

From here, turn right to go uphill again. The path joins a more clearly defined track, passing between two rows of bushes and trees.

Where the track forks (4), take the left fork down to the brook, head to the right, then cross the brook and follow the track uphill. At the T-junction of two paths (5), take the right-hand turn, towards the farm buildings.

At the farm, turn left (6) keeping the farm house on your right. Do not be tempted to follow the track: the *footpath* runs alongside the wall, on your left, as

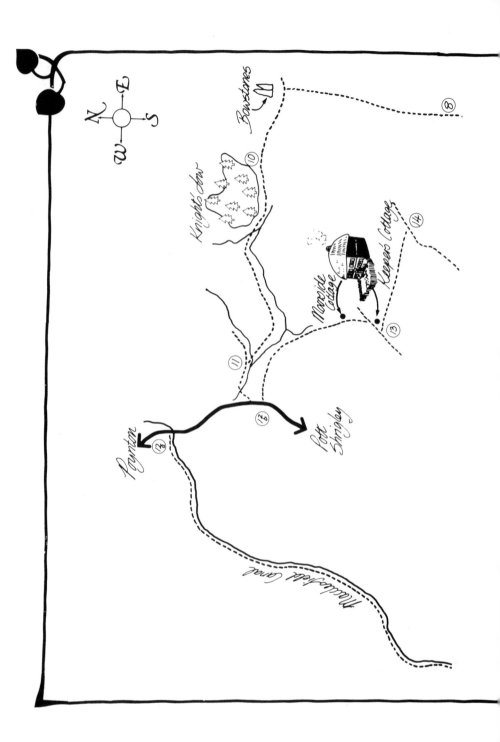

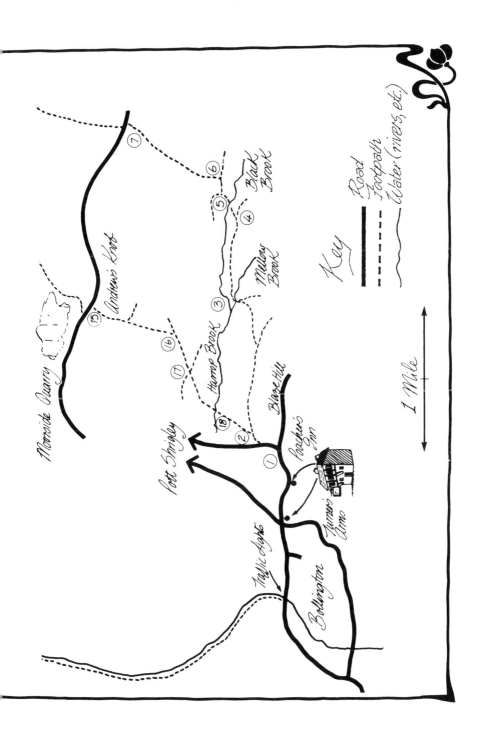

Key

Road
Footpath
Water (rivers, etc.)

1 Mile

Moorside Quarry

Andrew's Knot

Black Brook

Milnus Brook

Hump Brook

Pott Shrigley

Blaze Hill

Poacher's Inn

Turner's Arms

Traffic Lights

Bollington

55

far as the road.

At the road (7), turn left, then almost immediately right along a track leading directly to Bowstones. Enthusiasts should note that this is part of the Gritstone Trail. Along the track look out for the Viewfinder (8) (signposted, on your right)–a metal plate indicating the locations of surrounding hills and other prominent features.

The Bowstones (9) are two lumps of rock, to the right of Bowstones Farm. No one seems sure of their origin and they are surrounded by a fence so, if you came to see the Bowstones, you're liable to be disappointed.

Follow the signposted path to the left of Bowstones Farm into Lyme Park. Cross a ladder stile and, from here, you could well be rewarded by catching sight of the large numbers of deer in the park.

Follow the path towards Knight's Low (10), the large wooded area. When you reach it, turn left and follow the wall as far as a small stream. Cross this and again continue alongside the wall. If you peep over the first stile in this wall, you'll see Lyme Cage–a prominent folly.

As the main wall ends, turn left and walk to the left of a derelict house, with an equally ramshackle wall on your left. The path continues downhill, through the bracken until you reach a wide track by a stream (11).

Turn left here and continue to West Park Gate, where you turn left. Cross the bridge and turn right along the path to the road. From here, you have a choice–turn right and join the Macclesfield Canal (12a), where you turn left and follow the Tow Path back to Bollington–no instructions necessary. Or, shorter and more scenically, turn left and walk along the road until you reach the Methodist Chapel (12b). The path you need is the track to the right of the Chapel. Continue straight ahead, along the path between the first two cottages you reach. The path generally follows a fence, then a wall–keep this on your immediate left, as it will enable you to find the stiles.

As the wall dips away downhill, head right along a very well-defined path. As you head across open moorland, Moorside Cottage will be seen on your left, and Keeper's Cottage ahead and slightly to the right. Head for the stile in the top right hand corner of the field–turn right, then left after Keeper's Cottage, (signposted Bowstone Gates and Kettleshulme). Walk uphill alongside the wall, until you reach a stile. Cross this and head straight ahead, downhill. As the path levels out (after about 50 yards) turn right (14) and walk along a fairly obvious grassy track to the road–a distance of about half a mile.

Turn left at the road, walk uphill about 80 yards then turn right at the stile (15). Walk alongside the wall and then, at the top of the hill, continue in the same direction to walk alongside the next wall.

At the first stile you encounter turn right (16) and head downhill with the wood on your right and the wall on your left.

Where the path joins the farm drive (with a stone building on your right), cross the drive (17) and continue downhill in the same direction you have just travelled, making a 45 degree angle with the farm drive and dropping below the farm buildings.

Continue over a couple of rough planks laid over minor streams (at the time of writing) and find the stile set into a stone wall above and to the right of a larger stream.

Continue from here downhill to the packhorse bridge (18) which you cross and carry straight on, over the hill, to a stile about 100 yards to the left of the Cheshire Hunt (2).

Turn right here to the road, then left along the road and back to your starting point.

Bollington from White Nancy

This vigorous walk includes the most scenic surroundings of Bollington: Ingersley Vale, Big Low and Berristall Dale. Add to this an insight into Bollington's industrial past, and you have an ideal afternoon walk.

Walk along Church Street towards the factory facing you (1), then turn left and walk past Shrigley Dyers on your left and the pool on your right.

Continue along the track until about 50 yards or so after the last factory, where you cross a stile (2) into a field.

Go over the bridge and follow the grassy track which leads, at first, straight ahead, then climbs uphill to the left.

As you climb uphill, Big Low is the prominent hump in the landscape facing you. As you may know, "low" is Anglo Saxon for "hill". Part of the path you are on, you will notice, is roughly paved. This is a common feature of paths in the area, as they were used by millworkers walking from outlying villages.

Continue through the stiles, straight to the top of this hill where you will see a wide gateway with a stile adjacent (3). Cross this and turn right along the farm track.

After about a quarter of a mile, and before you reach the highest point on this track, turn left through a gate (4). Although unsigned this is easy enough to find – there is another gate almost opposite and the gateway that you must go through has a right-hand gatepost with three equally spaced holes through it.

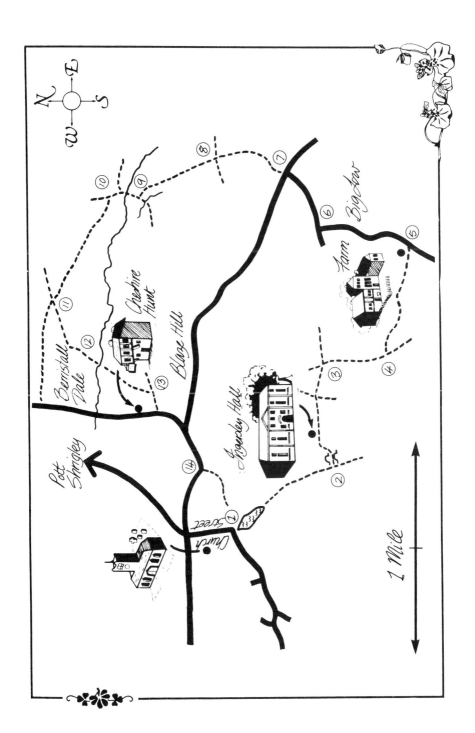

Walk into the field and keep the wall that is facing you on your left. The footpath is a well-defined track leading to a farm. *Note:* If you find this path too muddy for your liking, turn back and follow the original track to Lower House, then turn left along the road to Clarke House.

Go through the farmyard and turn left(5), along the very minor road, taking you past Big Low. From the top of this road, there are excellent views of Kerridge, White Nancy and Bollington on your left. Further away, Alderley Edge is clearly visible.

At a T-junction with another track (6) turn right and continue to the road, where you turn left, then almost immediately right, through a gate (7).

From here, carry straight on along a track ignoring the one on your left.

As the track continues downhill, you will see a stone-built property on your left (8). Immediately after this, cross the stile on your left and continue downhill – the path goes immediately to the right of a large hollybush and continues to the left of an overgrown hedge. At the end of the hedge, cross the field and head towards the farm building, where there is a stile in the fence (9). Cross the stile and turn right through a gate to head downhill to two footbridges. From the second footbridge, head uphill and to the right towards a stile. Cross this and continue a short distance to a track (10), where you turn left.

Continue along the track until you pass through a gate with a wood on your right and farm buildings straight ahead. What follows is the *only* tricky part of the walk – so be careful:

Almost exactly half way between the gate and the buildings (11), turn left at 45 degrees and head downhill. The path goes to the left of a telegraph pole and joins a small stream which runs from the farm buildings. At the time of writing, a rough footbridge (a thick plank) was thoughtfully placed across the stream. Cross the stream – probably dry in the summer – and turn left. The stile you require is set into the stone wall above and to the right of the stream.

From here, go straight ahead and downhill along a well used path. At the foot of the hill, go through a stile and over a packhorse bridge (12), which is one of the many attractive features of the Gritstone Trail.

From here, carry straight over the top of the hill and head for the pub facing you (The Cheshire Hunt). Leave the field by the stile 100 yards or so to the left of the pub (13), turn right along the track, then left at the road.

Walk along the road as far as the Poachers Arms (14), where you turn left and walk along Mill Lane, past the bowling green until you reach a minor road. You should recognise where you are now – turn right and head back to Church Street.

Walk: B4

Route: The Saddle of Kerridge

Starting Point: Chancery Lane, Bollington (SJ937775)

Length: Two and a half miles. Moderate.

Duration: One hour.

This is the shortest walk in the book, and is ideal for a summer evening's stroll, or as the basis for a longer walk. It includes the White Nancy monument, visible for miles around, so it's worth doing this walk just to satisfy your curiosity!

You can complete the walk – like any other in this book – in either direction. I chose to complete the steep part first – you may feel otherwise.

Parking the car can be a problem in that you may be unable to park precisely at the beginning (or end) of the walk which is at the easterly end of the row of terraced houses in Chancery Lane (1). To get your bearings, walk away from the Red Lion, at the end of High Street, and walk down Chancery Lane. The steps and footpath sign are on your right, at the end of the terrace.

White Nancy is clearly visible from here and the path is easy to follow – go through the first stile to a second one, where you turn right and straight up the hill to the monument. The view from the top is really impressive – particularly of Bollington, which is spread out like a map below you.

Walk along the ridge until you reach a stile, with the village of Rainow on the far left. Do not cross the stile – turn right and head downhill.

Cross the road, turn right then left down a track (4) running alongside the road. Follow the track, being careful to keep to the left of Endon House, and continue to the main road. Turn right here, then right again (3) at the stile just past the buildings. Follow the path across the field – this is one of the old paved mill worker's paths and is easy to follow.

Turn left where the path meets the road and walk downhill to the main road (6). Turn right here and right again at Redway, by the Bull's Head (7). At the Redway Tavern (8), on a sharp bend, take the footpath to the left of the Tavern and go straight ahead. Turn left at the next stile, walk down the steps and back to your starting point.

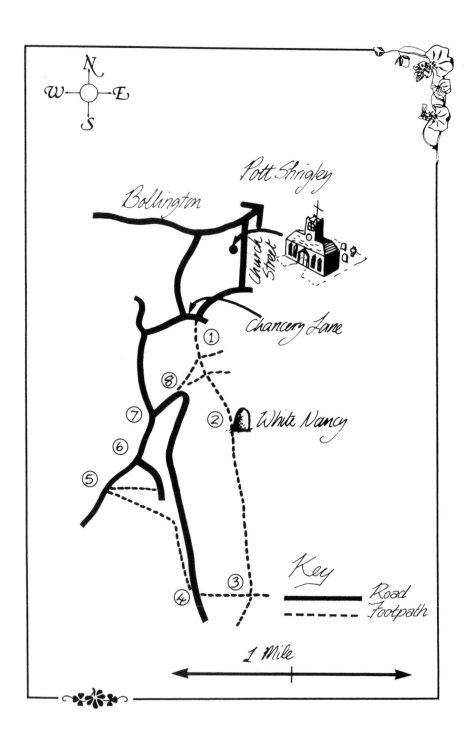

Pott Shrigley

Bollington

Church Street

Chancery Lane

White Nancy

① ⑧ ⑦ ⑥ ⑤ ② ③ ④

Key

Road

Footpath

1 Mile

Gawsworth, Wincle & Congleton

These two areas are combined simply because of their proximity. The scenery and type of walking are, however, quite different.

Gawsworth's main claim to fame is the Old Hall, dating from the late 15th Century. It has belonged to a succession of families, most notably the Fittons (1662 to 1702). Mary Fitton is said to be the "Dark Lady" of Shakespeare's sonnets, and the Shakespearean connection continues today with the season of outdoor plays. The hall itself is open from Easter to October.

The New Hall is now used as council offices, its Georgian style forming an interesting contrast to the black-and-white Old Hall. It is particularly impressive from the drive between the two halls, as you walk past the statues and ornamental fish ponds. The New Hall achieved some notoriety when its original owner, Lord Mohun, lost his life in one of the last duels fought in England. The stewards at the duel were accused of being accomplices to murder.

The odd-shaped house between the two halls is known as The Watch Tower. One possible reason for its existence was to overlook the surrounding lands and forest, though some believe that its thick walls might suggest that it was also used as some sort of prison.

Wincle is quite different. Whereas Gawsworth lies in mainly flat farmland, Wincle stands amid the hills above the Dane valley. Useful places to know about are The Ship Inn and the nearby trout farm.

Although Wincle does not have such architectural claims to fame as Gawsworth, it is just as popular though its visitors tend to wear hiking boots rather than high-heeled shoes.

The Walks

Of all the areas covered in this book, these must rank as favourites. The area around Wincle, in particular, is just hilly enough to be stimulating, but without losing its greenness as do some of the wilder parts of the Peak District. A section of the Gritstone Trail passes through Wincle and that, of course, is included. Most walkers from Wincle normally cross the Dane into Derbyshire, but the walk suggested here is a purely Cheshire affair.

Walk: GWC1

Route: Gawsworth and North Rode.

Starting Point: Road adjacent to St. James Church, Gawsworth (SJ890698)

Length: Six miles. Easy.

Duration: Two and a half hours.

My main memory of Gawsworth is the annual Shakespearean season, performed outdoors on Summer evenings in the grounds of the Old Hall. Even if your knowledge of The Bard is abysmal as mine, you should not miss it – there can be scarcely anything more English.

But, here is a chance to see the surrounding countryside – although quite flat, the scenery is as English as the Shakespearean performances, and you can easily fit this walk into a summer evening. There is a stretch of road to be walked, but you'll find that it's normally quiet.

Parking at a precise spot can be a minor problem around here – it is so justifiably popular. Our walk begins at Gawsworth Church (1) but you'll easily find a nearby place to leave the car.

Walk past the church, on your left. (If you have time, pop inside – the church dates back over 500 years and you can see the splendid monuments and effigies of the Fitton family including that of Mary Fitton, mentioned in the introduction to this section.

Leaving the church on your left, walk along the lane and turn left at the "North Rode" signpost, over a stile, into a field, after which the footpath continues straight ahead.

The hill ahead of you, by the way is Bosley Cloud – a very recognisable landmark. Also, more to your left, you'll see the Sutton Common radio mast, a prominent feature on the Gritstone Trail.

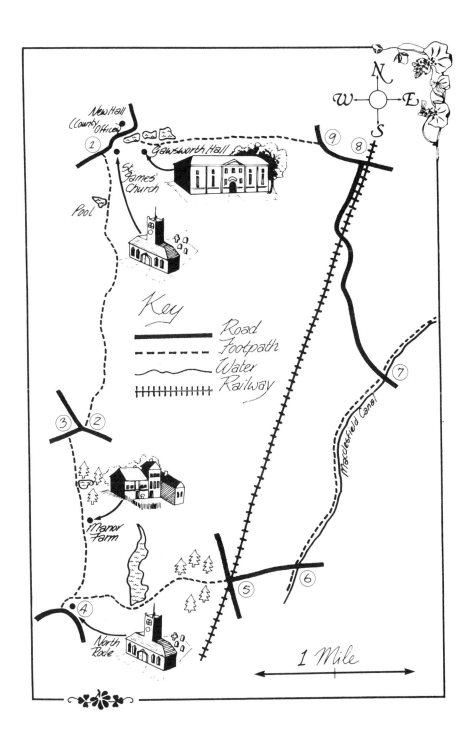

Key

Road
Footpath
Water
Railway

New Hall (County Offices)
Gawsworth Hall
St James' Church
Pool
Manor Farm
North Rode
Macclesfield Canal

1 Mile

After crossing the third of three more stiles, against a holly hedge you should fork left to head for the next stile. Cross this and continue straight across the next field to its top left corner. Cross the stile and walk alongside the fence – the path now continues virtually straight ahead through a series of stiles to the road (2), which you cross. Carry on down Pexall Road, turn left at the North Rode sign (3) and continue straight ahead to Manor Farm. The path is to the right of the main farm buildings, and crosses a stile just to the left of a small brick barn (the building on the extreme right).

Continue straight ahead from here along the farm drive.

At the end of the drive, you go over a cattle grid and face a cottage (4). Turn left here, walk along a drive, cross a stile into a field and continue alongside the fence on your right. Leave the field by the next stile, turn right and follow the park drive.

At the end of the drive, cross over the railway bridge (5) and follow the road until the canal bridge. Turn left (6) and follow the towpath until bridge number 51, where you turn left (7) to join a country road.

Follow the road (not the farm track on the left) to a T-junction, where you turn left to Gawsworth (9). Just after a farm on your left, fork left along a signposted track, through a series of kissing gates and stiles, back to Gawsworth. This part of the walk takes you between picturesque cottages and the lake in front of the new hall, now used as County offices. If the Old Hall is open, change your hiking books and soak up some local history; you'll find it well worth while.

Gawsworth Hall (By permission, Cheshire Life)

Walk: GWC2

Route: Wincle to Sutton Common, along the Gritstone Trail.

Starting Point: Roadside above The Ship Inn, Wincle (SJ962653).

Length: Nine and a half miles. Moderate/Strenuous.

Duration: Four hours.

The Gritstone Trail is one of the most famous cross-country walks and it can easily be completed along its entire 20 mile length in one day, from Rushton Spencer to Lyme Park. If, however, you fancy a circular walk that includes just part of the trail, here's your chance.

Walk uphill from The Ship and after 50 yards climb a flight of stone steps on your left (1). Cross the field to the opposite stile, to the right of the farm buildings then cross a stone stile and follow the stone wall on your left. At the end of this wall cross the stile and head through the wood, uphill, over another stile, to a stile slightly to your right which emerges onto a lane.

Turn left and follow the lane until you are about 30 yards from the main entrance to Wincle Grange Farm (2). The ecclesiastical style of the farm buildings is deliberate – the farm was established by an order of monks. Turn left through a gate and follow a path with a prefabricated barn on your left and the farm buildings on your right. Leave the farmyard through the gate and head diagonally downhill, aiming just to the left of the junction of a fence and an overgrown hedge. Continue straight ahead from here, into the corner of the field, then follow the hedge (on your right) downhill.

At the stile level with a farm on your right (3), turn right through a gate, then left and continue downhill. The high ridge ahead of you is Wincle Minn, which is on the route to Croker Hill.

Head straight downhill and you will find a fence running alongside the stream. At the extreme left hand corner of this fence, a smaller stream joins the main one. Cross the main stream just below the junction of these streams. Follow the line of the power cables and you'll see a stile on the horizon. Cross this and follow the cables until the next pole. From here, the path leaves the line of cables on the left and follows a path above a wood on your right, with a farm straight ahead in the distance.

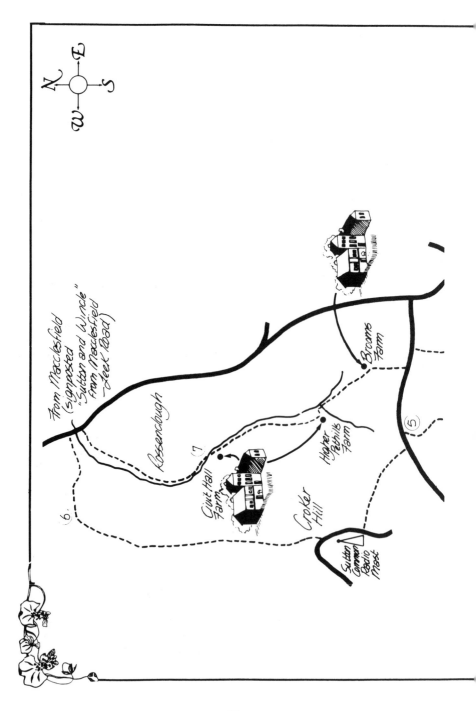

From Macclesfield
(signposted
"Sutton and Wincle"
from Macclesfield
— Leek Road)

Rossenclough

Giant Hall Farm

7

Croker Hill

Higher Pethills Farm

Brook Farm

5

6

Sutton Common Radio Mast

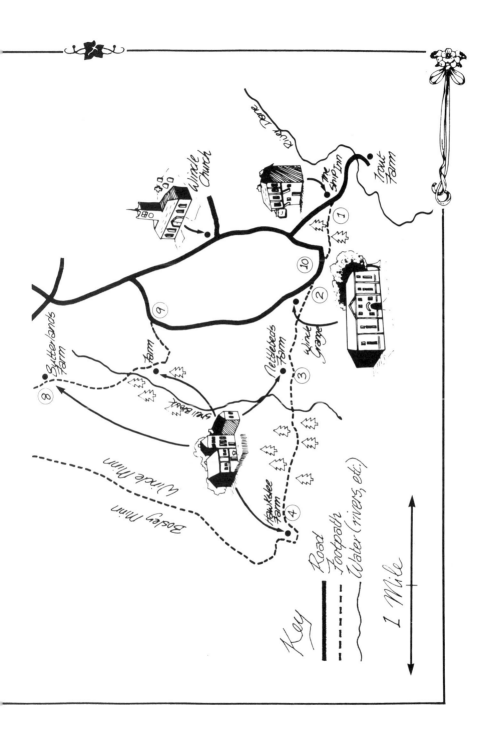

Key

Road
Footpath
Water (rivers, etc.)

1 Mile

Follow the path to the extreme end of the wood, on your left. Pass the gate at this point and follow the grassy track towards the farm.

To be correct, this path now continues straight ahead, to the right of Hawkslee Farm but it can be very muddy and the farmer has kindly arranged a concessionary path, as follows:

Just before the large barn on your right (4), fork left, cross over a small stream and over a stile. Now go uphill to the stile midway between a bungalow and the farm, where you turn right and follow the Gritstone Trail (a surfaced track along this stretch) until you reach the road (5).

Turn left and follow the road until you reach a stile on your right. Cross this and follow the hedge on your left. Cross a stile and head uphill towards the Sutton Common telecommunications mast – the route is obvious and well waymarked; it joins a track through a stile to the right of a farm building.

Turn right here and follow the track past the radio mast.

After about 100 yards, the path leaves this main track and forks right along a well-used but often boggy route. You are now back on the Gritstone Trail and the path lies straight ahead – just follow the waymarks with the familiar Gritstone symbol (G). The only thing to watch out for is that, after the right hand turn (6) leading to the road, the path forks gently to the right and away from the wall on your left – it is in any event, a well-walked track and you *should* not miss it.

Turn right at the road, then right again along the drive to Kinderfields Farm. Follow the track, passing "Rossenclough" (marked on the map as Redwood Farm) on your left.

Eventually, you cross a cattle grid at the entrance to Civit Hills (also called Civit Hall) Farm (7). After about 50 yards, cross the fence – at present, there is no stile, only a rusty old gate and a section of un-barbed wire. Head towards the stream and follow it upstream towards an old but more serviceable, stile than the apology that you just scrambled over! (Maybe a decent one has been installed by now – in which case, my apologies). Carry on through the next "stile" – at present an old gate tied up with baler twine. Continue upstream and cross a smaller tributary coming in from the right. About 100 yards later, the path leaves the stream and heads uphill, following the hedge on your right.

Soon, the path crosses a stile and heads straight to Higher Pethills Farm, – passing between the two main buildings. Turn left here, then cross a stile a few yards before the farm gate, alongside the stream. The path runs alongside the fence and hedge on your right and continues towards the next farm.

Keep just to the right of this farm, then turn right onto its drive and head for the road. Turn left here, then right to Butterlands Farm (8).

Go through the farmyard, then through a wooden gate, leading into a field with a fence on your left. Continue straight ahead, go through the next gateway and go down the ridge of the hill, leading to the stream which is below you and to the left.

At the foot of the hill, cross a stile into a wood and follow the path down to the stream. You should aim to cross the stream just downstream of where a smaller stream enters from the opposite side. The banks are steep and often slippery here. On my last visit, I noticed that preparations were in hand for new fencing and, hopefully, stiles will be installed to guide you.

Having crossed the stream, head uphill at a 45 degree angle to the stream along a well-used path which crosses the fence by way of a rudimentary stile.

Now follow the fence on your right, past a farm that has seen better days, and then fork right after the farm to a stile some 50 yards to the left of a Dutch barn.

Turn left at the stile and follow the farm track. At the point where the track joins a minor road (9), turn right and head for Wincle Grange. Pass through the farm, then past a pool on your right and head downhill. After about 150 yards, cross a stone stile on your right (10). Enter the field and head for the wood, your path making an angle of 45 degrees with the wall on your left. Cross the stile and head through the wood, rejoining the original path that you followed when starting the walk.

Walk: GWC3
Route: Timbersbrook, The Cloud, Rushton Spencer, and the Bridestones
Starting Point: Timbersbrook Picnic Site (SJ895627)
Length: 7½ miles. Easy/Moderate
Duration: 3½ hours

This "East Cheshire" walk is a bit of a cheat: it starts in Cheshire, but most of it is in Staffordshire! The problem I had was that it seemed a good idea to include a walk up The Cloud but – having got there – where to go? A glance at the map shows that the only logical route is east, towards Rushton Spencer and Staffordshire – and none the worse for that. On the return journey a neolithic burial chamber is included, to add a spot of culture.

Leave the car at Timbersbrook Picnic Site (1) – once the centre of a thriving little hamlet based on a silk mill. Walk from the car park *through* the picnic site then turn left up Tunstall Road. After a while, turn right (2) along Gosberry Hole Lane, all the way to a National Trust sign. This section is easy – just walk along an obvious track, forking left at the plantation (3) and admire the open views on your left as you stroll up to the trig point. From here, carry on in the direction you've been walking, heading downhill along the track which ends in an over-civilised flight of concrete steps. Turn left here and go down a track to the road.

At the road, turn left (4), walk downhill and then turn right at a stile bearing the 'knot' sign for the Staffordshire Way. Follow a wall on your right along a well-used and waymarked path, eventually joining a minor road (5) to the right of a farm.

Bear right here and follow the road to Ravensclough Farm (6). Turn right before the farm and aim for the edge of the wood. The path runs through the wood and then crosses a stream. From here, cross a meadow, heading just to the right of a copse, and on towards the railway bridge. Cross another stream and turn right onto the disused railway track (7) to Rushton Spencer.

Cross the road – this leads you to the Knot Inn at Rushton Spencer (8) – a good place to wine and dine, at the right time. Traditionally, it's also the start of the Gritstone Trail. Our path passes between the Knot and the old station on the right. Walk along the old track and under a large stone arch bridge. Go left up the steps of this bridge and cross over the track, which means that you have actually turned *right*, following a path to the church of St. Laurence (10); this intriguing building has a small wooden tower and gravestones dating back to 1610. It is set in a lonely, beautiful stretch of countryside but is – regrettably – usually locked; a sign of the times.

Go through the church yard to a track, crossing over a minor road to a stile. Continue straight ahead to a further stile adjacent to a gate and then head slightly right to the top corner of the field, where you should find a small pond. Go round the edge of the pond (11) until you reach a stile, then head uphill with the hedge on your left. The path then takes you past Ditchway Farm on your right, over a stile and along a farm drive to the road, where you turn left (12).

From here, there's some unavoidable road walking – so take care.

Follow the minor road, keeping left at the first junction until you reach the main Congleton road. Turn right and, after about 300 yards, you reach Bridestones – a Neolithic burial chamber. (*Note*: the entrance to the Bridestones is *after* the house of the same name.) You'll find a placard to tell you a little about it – but the most impressive aspect is its size. Its discovery was somewhat accidental – if you look around the immediate vicinity, you'll see that many of the chamber rocks were used to construct garden walls until the archaeological significance of the site was recognised. There are many such burial chambers around here – look with suspicion on any large hump in the ground, but don't start excavating; you would not only be a vandal, but also in clear breach of the law.

The footpath situation from here is a little odd and I have explored it fairly exhaustively. One path leads north from Bridestones, but ends in no-man's land. Second best is to continue towards Congleton and take the first turn right to Cloud Park Farm; a path does then lead off to the left from the farm drive, but ends in a tangle of barbed wire. Third best is to swallow your pride and continue further along the Congleton road to the next farm after Cloud Park, namely Smithy Farm (13).

Here, turn right into the farmyard, then fork left towards a wooded area. A clear path alongside and above a stream passes through a stile, then down towards a dip, where it crosses over the stream. From here head up to a stile in the wall (14). Turn right and follow the road back to the car.

If you find a better legal alternative to this last bit – let me know!

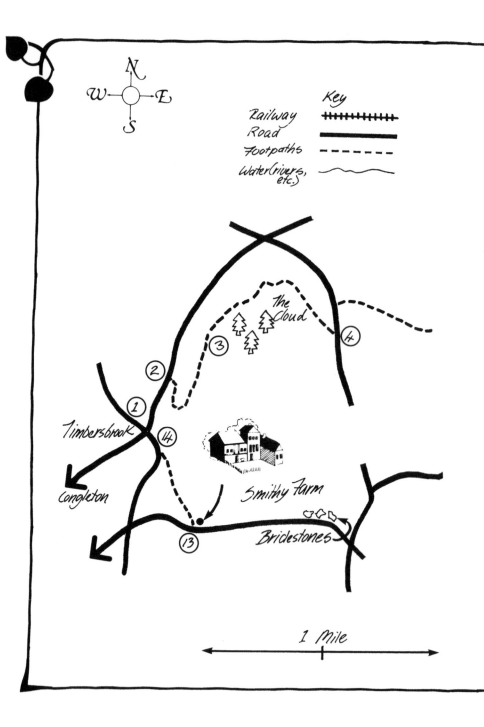

Key

Railway
Road
Footpaths
Water (rivers, etc.)

N
W — E
S

The Cloud

② ③
④
① ⑭

Timbersbrook

Congleton

Smithy Farm

⑬

Bridlestones

1 Mile

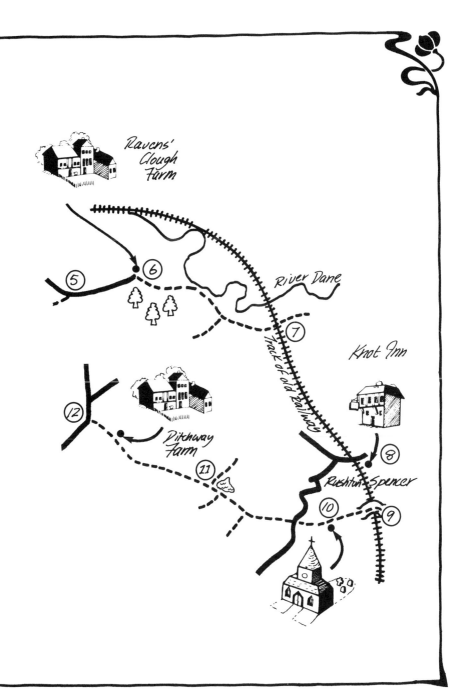

Ravens'
Clough
Farm

⑤ ⑥

River Dane

⑦

Track of old Railway

Knot Inn

⑫

Ditchway
Farm

⑪

Rushton Spencer

⑧

⑩

⑨

The Peak National Park boundary – on the Macclesfield to Buxton road

Kettleshulme and Rainow

These are hill-country villages, better known now as centres for walking than for their previous industrial importance.

Like many of the surrounding towns and villages, these two reached their peak in the late 19th and early 20th Centuries. At one time, Rainow alone had 13 mills and 9 public houses. The mills were of various types – silk, cotton and fustian – even a candlewick mill at Lumb Hole, Rainow, on the banks of Todd Brook. A large proportion of the population was home-based, weaving at small looms in their cottages. The materials for this cottage industry were obtained from nearby Macclesfield or Bollington, thus explaining the numerous and unusual paved footpaths that cross the open countryside. There are no surviving mills – the last one, the Swan Vale in Kettleshulme, closed as recently as 1979.

Apart from weaving, another major industry was engineering – both in its own right and as a service to local farmers. Surprisingly, the engineering was of the heavy variety, producing steam rollers, steam hammers and the like. One of the local stories is of John Mellor, a Rainow engineer who manufactured steam rollers. One of his early models became stuck in one of Rainow's muddy fields, much to the delight of local farmers who offered to remove it with their "more dependable" horses. Mr. Mellor refused, insisted that he would drive his roller out of the mud – and he did.

Both the weaving and engineering declined as Macclesfield and Stockport increased in importance. Quarrying continued until relatively recently, up to 1000 men being employed in the industry at one time. Nowadays, hill farming is the order of the day, though few of the farms appear to be very prosperous. Perhaps the largest local undertaking is Lamaload reservoir: the North West Water Board owns large tracts of land locally, but its employees are few in number – water has a habit of looking after itself!

The Walks

This is a stimulating area for walkers. The scenery is superb, including small lowland farms, tumbling streams and rugged hills. The most impressive stretch of hill walking is along the Tors (Shining Tor, Cat's Tor along to Pym Chair) which separates Cheshire from Derbyshire). The entire area, including the Water Board land, is criss-crossed by a superb network of paths.

Walk: KR1

Route: Lamaload, The Tors and Pym Chair.

Starting Point: Car Park, East of Lamaload reservoir (SJ976753).

Length: Seven miles. Moderate/Strenuous.

Duration: Three and a half hours.

This magnificent walk is reminiscent of some of the finest Welsh hill walking – a rare compliment as far as I am concerned. Although the hills are steep, the paths are easy to find, giving you plenty of time to admire the views.

Access to the car park is usually from the junction with the A5002 (see map) and is signposted to the Goyt Valley. On your way down the road, look out for the small stone memorial describing the dastardly deed of over 200 years ago when one John Turner was found dead in the snow in suspicious circumstances. From the car park, go back to the road and turn right. Turn left at the bridge (1), along a grassy track signposted to "Burbage and Shining Tor". The path goes steeply uphill, alongside a stream. As the stream runs slightly to the right, continue straight ahead to a stile. From here, follow the track and head for a large gap roughly mid-way along a stone wall on the skyline.

At the wall (2), fork right and converge on the wall to your right. Now, simply follow the wall. Some fine views open out ahead of you, including Shutlingsloe from about point (3) on the map, where the path levels out. The Sutton Common tower is also clearly visible, slightly to your right.

Cross the stile and head straight up the steep hill to Shining Tor (5). To visit the triangulation point, you need to head to the right and follow the track to a stile on your right: the trig point is actually on private land, but concessionary access is provided.

Now, follow the broad – almost straight – track all the way to Cat's Tor and Pym Chair. If you have chosen to do this walk at any time but high summer, you'll quickly discover what a soggy place this can be, and why many seasoned walkers can be seen in wellies!

At the end of the ridge, turn left along a road taking you past Pym Chair. If you object to using this road, or to make a somewhat longer walk, you can divert along footpaths to the left or right at about point (7) on the map. You will, however, need to consult an O.S. map so that you end up at our common destination, Jenkin Chapel (8). Follow the path opposite to the chapel signposted to Rainow. Head directly away from the chapel, over the hill and towards a barn at the foot of the hill.

Cross a rather indistinct stile in the stone wall some 50 yards before the corner in the wall. Then, cross the footbridge (9). Alternatively, turn right at the wall and take your chance over the stream.

Turn right behind the barn (10) – do not go as far as the footbridge – and walk uphill, following a wall at first, then the remains of a hedge. Cross this stile and head slightly to the right over a stile into a wood (11). Follow the obvious path to a stile in the top right hand corner of the wood.

Follow the path alongside a wall, cross over a stile and find the next stile – straight ahead – at the road (12).

Turn left here, then right after about 100 yards at a gate (13). Walk along the track, passing behind a farmhouse en route; Lamaload is now clearly in sight, on your left.

From this farmhouse, follow the track to a short, tumbledown wall which you keep on your left – the next stile is in the corner of the wall facing you. Cross the stile and head to the next farm – Common Barn (14) – keeping the wall on your right.

Cross the farmyard and follow the wall on your right as far as the next stile (15), where you turn left. When you arrive at a gate and stile (16) head downhill with the copse and building on your right. A well-used path takes you towards the water treatment works.

At the stile behind the Water Board houses (17), turn left by 45 degrees and head up hill, passing through a prominent gap in the wall near the top of the hill. Head to the right from here and join a track with the wall on your right, all the way back to the car park.

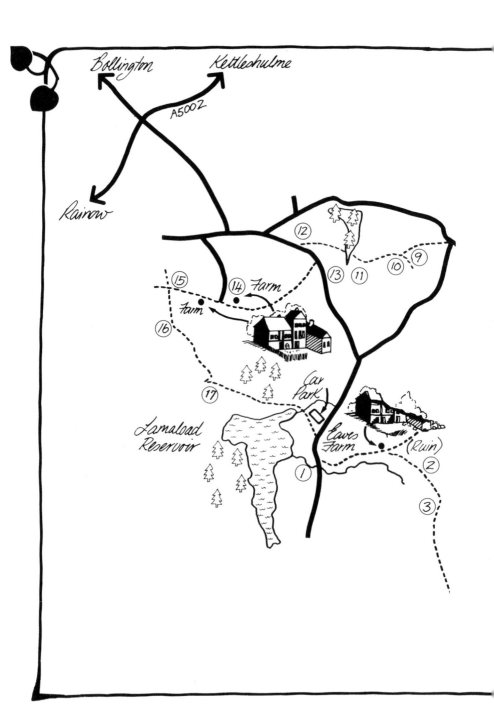

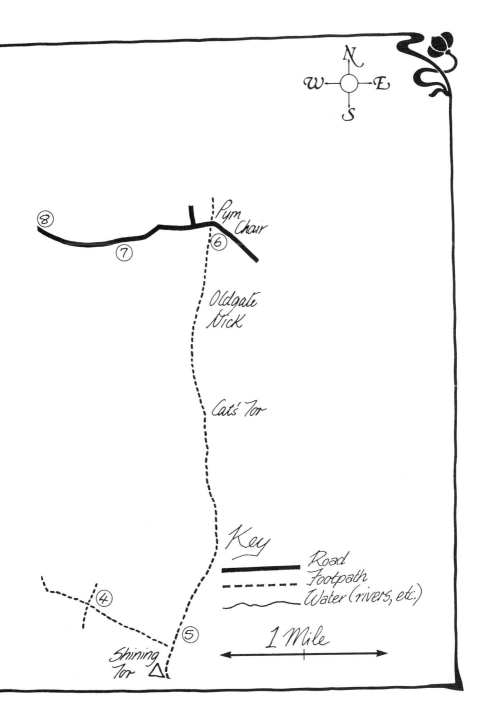

N
W E
S

⑧
⑦
⑥ Pym Chair

Oldgate Nick

Cat's Tor

Key

Road
Footpath
Water (rivers, etc.)

④
⑤

Shining Tor △

1 Mile

This takes you through some quite isolated and beautiful countryside – yet so accessible for a motorist lucky enough to own a pair of boots.

Depending on how energetic you feel, you may wish to complete just this walk or to link up with Walk KR3 which takes you over to Macclesfield Forest.

Walk from the car park towards the reservoir, along the path to the right of a large stone building. Turn right after about 30 yards and walk down a track to a stile (1).

This leads along a path over the hill and through a large gap in the wall, towards the Water Board houses (2) near to the dam.

Follow the path down the hill, passing the footpath signs pointing to where you have just been. At the foot of the hill, turn left, and cross a stream.

Walk along a track, between a pair of stone walls. Just before a gate, fork right along a paved path, then turn left at the Water Board's road and walk along this for about one mile, passing firstly Snipe House Farm (3) and then Higherlane Farm (4).

The road now dips (5) – as it rises again, Bollington and White Nancy are visible straight ahead. Fifty yards after the second building on your left after Higher Lane Farm, cross a stone stile set into the wall and head diagonally to your left (6), crossing the stone wall near to the back gate to the house on your left.

Continue in the same direction, uphill. Be sure to keep the walls on your left and right at roughly equal distances; you will find a rather worse-for-wear stile in the wall facing you. Continue uphill, with the wall on your immediate right.

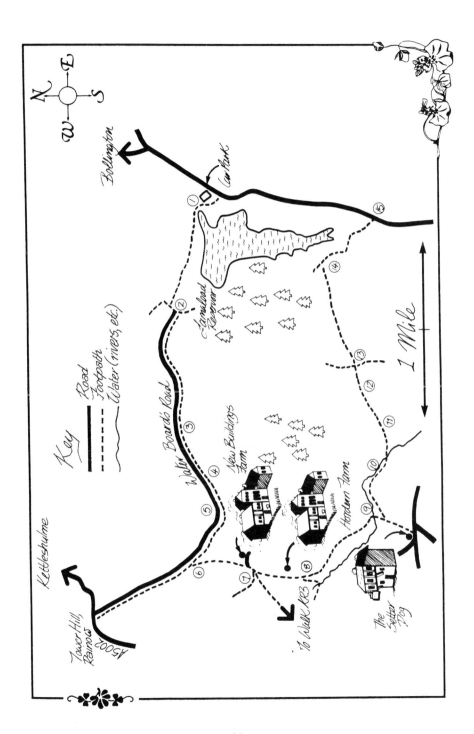

Key

Road
Footpath
Water (rivers, etc.)

Bollington

Car Park

Lamaload Reservoir

Water Board's Road

New Buildings Farm

Horden Farm

The Setter Dog

To Walk KR3

Kettleshulme

Tower Hill, Rainow

A5002

1 Mile

83

Just before a tumbledown wall, there is an equally tumbledown stile on your right. Cross this and again head uphill, with the wall initially on your immediate left. As it drops away, you carry on in the direction you are heading, as far as a stile adjacent to gate (7).

Turn right here, walking along the farm track. Continue along the track until you reach Hordern Farm. Cross the stile in the wall adjacent to a gate (8) which you see as you are leaving the last farm building on your left. Walk along this well-used track, with the wall on your left. This track (through "Gulshaw Hollow") is easy to follow. Continue to a stile which leads across a stream (9).

Go uphill about 100 yards and turn left along a farm track. Walk past a near-derelict farmhouse, then follow the track over a stream and past a small building on your left (10). From here, head left with the wall on your left. After the wall has bent to the right you will see a stone stile. Cross this and continue in the same direction – head over the hill using the wall on the skyline (11) as your marker. From here, carry straight on to another stile set in a wall, and likewise to the next one.

After crossing the hill, the next stile is a wooden one in the top right hand corner of the field (12). Cross this and head along a path making an approximately 45 degree angle with the stream. This takes you off again in roughly the same direction of travel as before.

Cross the farm drive (13) and enter the next field through the gateway or nearby stile. Continue straight ahead, with the wall on your right. After the next stile, either jump the stream and risk wet feet, or make a slight diversion to your right. Again, just carry straight on with the wall on your right.

Cross two derelict walls and Lamaload will soon appear out on your left – so long as there have been no more droughts.

Carry on down hill, turn right at the track (14) then left at the road (15) which leads you back to the car park.

Walk: KR3 (Continuation of Walk KR2)

Route: Lamaload, Teggs Nose and Langley.

Starting Point: Car Park, East of Lamaload Reservoir (SJ976753)

Length: Six miles, or ten and a half miles if Walk KR2 is included. Moderate/Strenuous

Duration: Two and a half hours (or five hours)

This is intended as an extension to Walk KR2, hence the points on the map are lettered, not numbered, to avoid confusion with the numbered KR2 map. However, there are two options:

If you would like to complete just this walk and not to include Walk KR2, this is quite easy: you will need to park your car either near to point (b) on the map (i.e. on the A537) or, perhaps, at the Setter Dog, which is easier so long as you square it with the landlord. If you do park at the pub, you can avoid a hazardous walk along the A537 by the following subterfuge:

(i) Walk down the track to the right of the Setter Dog.

(ii) Cross the stream at the bottom of the track and turn left over a stile.

(iii) Walk along Gulshaw Hollow until you reach Hordern Farm Pottery.

(iv) Turn left along the farm drive and walk up to the A537. From here, turn right and connect up with point (b) on the map.

If you wish to link this walk up with walk KR2, the idea is to leave that walk at point number (7), complete walk KR3, then rejoin the previous walk at point number (8). If this is the case, carry straight on at (7), rather than walking to Hordern Farm. This is part of the Gritstone Trail and is waymarked. From here, be sure to keep the wall on your right – do not follow the farm drive. At the top of the hill, go through a gate and continue in the same direction with the wall on your left.

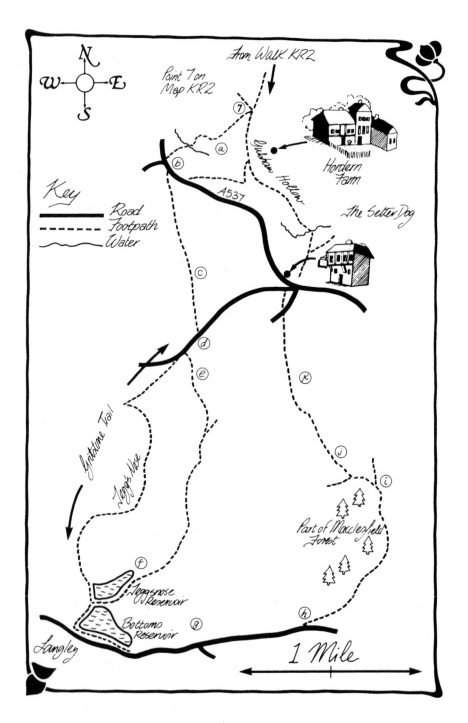

Head downhill and turn right on reaching the next wall (a). Do not go through the gate – instead, follow this wall until you reach a stile on your left. Cross this and head downhill to the stream. Go over this, turn left at the waymark and head uphill until you reach the road (A537).

Turn left here and walk uphill for a few yards, then cross the road to point (b).

Point (b) is our common starting point, being identified by a short flight of stone steps and a signpost to Tegg's Nose. Continue straight ahead and up the hill. The stiles are easy to find and they even have waymarks – a rare phenomenon.

As you approach the top of the hill you will pass a single wall on your left (c) – very obvious because it has no junction at its southerly end with any other wall. Cross the stile near this wall, then walk across the field and head for the next stile set mid-way in the wall facing you. Carry on straight ahead and you will see Tegg's Nose car park a few hundred yards in front of you.

Keep straight on, over two more stiles until arriving at a road (d). Turn right here, towards Tegg's Nose car park. From here, there are two possible routes: straight ahead (signposted Croker Hill) along a path initially parallel with the road; this is a continuation of the Gritstone Trail. Alternatively, go into the car park and find the "Viewpoint" plaque (e) which identifies all the surrounding hills.

Assuming that you are not descending by the Gritstone route (which I'll leave you to find), start from the Viewpoint and follow the footpath downhill (signposted to Langley), which levels out to join a rough road. At a crossroads, take the right fork, again signposted "Langley", (do not go as far as the farmhouse straight ahead).

The path now climbs slightly before dropping down again: take care not to branch off to the right – the path you want runs alongside the wall.

Cross over the stream, go uphill a short way, and join a track which leads to Tegg's Nose Reservoir (f), on your right.

At the far end of the reservoir, turn left and walk along the path alongside Bottoms Reservoir. Follow the path around the reservoir, until you reach the road.

Turn left here, walk along the road and up the hill to the Leather's Smithy pub (g).

Fork left at the pub, continuing uphill. As you go over the top of the hill (about one third of a mile), the outskirts of Macclesfield Forest are visible with a track leading from the road to the left, into the forest.

Just after the entrance to the forest track (h) take a left turn (signposted "Walker Barn") to join the track, which is so easy to follow, no explanation is necessary.

Eventually, as the path levels out, you'll see an old building (i) at the fork, of two tracks. Take the left fork, walking past the old building on your immediate right. After about 100 yards, fork right along a minor path through the woods – there is a small "Walker Barn" signpost here.

The path emerges from the wood to meet a road. Cross the road and walk along the drive to the house (j) facing you. Pass between two buildings and cross the stile. Turn left at this stile and cross another stile in the left hand corner of the field. From here, the path lies straight ahead – just keep the stone wall that faces you on your immediate right. Tegg's Nose is now quite a sight, on your left.

As the ground dips slightly downhill, you cross a stream and continue in the same direction along a path which turns to the right of an old wall. The path continues almost straight ahead, passing below Warrilowhead Farm (k) and heading for a stile towards the left of the first group of buildings.

Turn right here and head for the main road, where you might have timed it right for a visit to the Setter Dog.

If not – and presuming you are linking up with walk KR2 – cross the road and follow the track to the right of the pub. This bends around to the right, where it meets a gateway leading towards the farm. From here, continue along walk KR2 starting between point numbers 9 and 10, which will take you back to Lamaload.

If you are not linking up with walk KR2, you could well be back at your starting place by now. At the very worst, you'll need to get back to point (b), for which see the directions at the beginning of this walk.

Walk: KR4

Route: Pym Chair, Charles Head and Windgather Rocks

Starting Point: Pym Chair (SJ996766)

Length: Seven miles. Moderate/Strenuous

Duration: Two and a half hours

It is so difficult to choose a favourite walk. And yet, this one, though it includes a small amount of road-walking, must be counted as one of my great favourites. Perhaps this is because of its variety – fields, streams, hills, forests and rocky outcrops – but also because of the splendid views from Charles Head and Taxal Edge. See if you agree!

The map for this walk indicates where you need to leave the A5002 Kettleshulme to Rainow road. It is signposted to Saltersford and Goyt Valley, almost opposite Blaze Hill coming up from Bollington.

Follow this road and eventually turn left – again signed to Goyt Valley. Continue past Jenkin Chapel to the top of the hill and you'll see the car park sign for Pym's Chair on your left.

Walk out of the car park (1), and turn left towards the T-junction. Turn right here and head back to Jenkin Chapel (2). If you must avoid roads at all costs, you can work out a footpath route, starting with the path near to Pymchair Farm, but it is hardly worth while.

Go past the chapel, straight ahead along a minor road (i.e. do not turn left here). Go down a steep hill, then up the other side until, just after passing a wood on your left, you'll see a stile on your right (3).

Cross this and follow the wall on your right to the next stile. Cross it and turn immediately left, now keeping the wall on your left. Cross another stile and continue downhill until almost at the bottom, where you turn right, with a stream on your left.

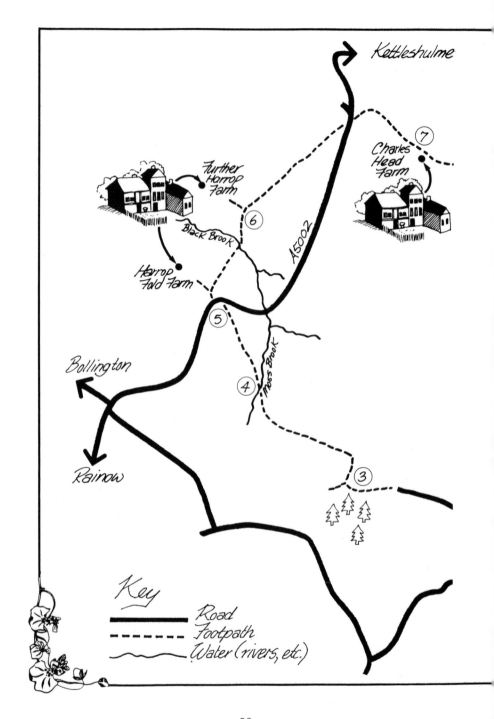

Kettleshulme

Charles
Head
Farm
⑦

Further
Harrop
Farm

Black Brook

⑥

A5002

Harrop
Fold Farm

⑤

Bollington

Moss Brook

④

Rainow

③

Key

Road
Footpath
Water (rivers, etc.)

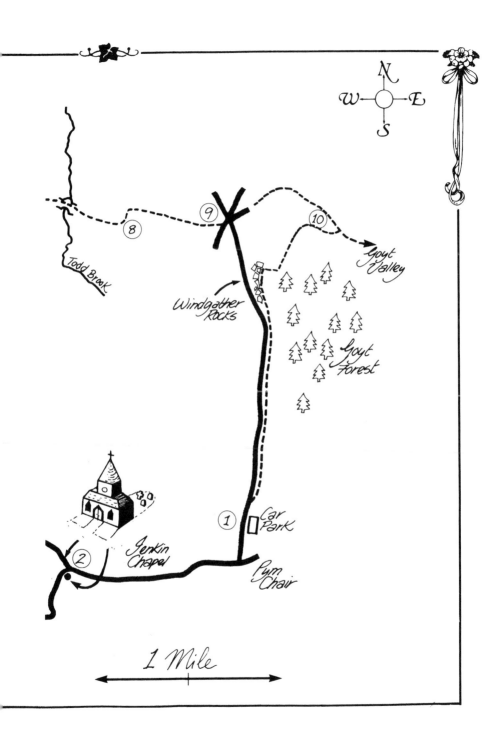

Cross the stream where it meets the wall (4) in the bottom right hand corner of the field. Then cross a smaller stream and carry on, in roughly the same direction as before, with the wall on your left. When you come to the end of this wall, you will find a rather messy collection of fencing, old gates and broken down walls, but no stile as such. Get through this lot as best you can and continue with the wall on your *right* hand side; continue along a track to the road (5).

Cross this busy road with care, walk uphill a short distance, then turn right along the drive to Harrop Fold Farm. Then, after about 30 yards, fork right and cross the stile adjacent to a gate. Now, follow a track which crosses Black Brook. At the top of the uphill stretch turn right (6), and follow a wall on your left for a short distance. Then, fork right and walk between two rows of trees until you reach the road.

Cross the road and continue along the track, towards Charles Head Farm (7). The Northerly views, to your left, are particularly impressive on this stretch of the walk. On a clear day, Whaley Moor, Chinley Churn and Kinder Scout can be seen.

Jenkin Chapel, Saltersford

Keep just to the left of the farm buildings, then follow a rough downhill track to a stile. From this stile, head straight down the hill to a footbridge over Todd Brook. As you walk down this hill, Windgather Rocks are prominent on the skyline – and that's where you're heading for!

Cross the bridge and follow the track uphill, then aim just to the right of an old house which is straight ahead. Turn left, through a gateway, with the house on your left (8) and head for the next house. Go through a gateway and turn right along a track to the right of this house.

Continue straight ahead (and mostly up!) towards the farm buildings to the left of Windgather. Turn left here to the appropriately-named Fivelane Ends (9). Cross the road junction, then fork right along a signposted track. This goes past an old house, then into a field. Fork slightly to your right and keep the wall on your right and carry straight on, over a stile. Turn sharp right here (10) over a stile into a conifer wood. (Before doing so, if the weather is good, just keep going for a few more yards for the view over the top of the hill – quite a breathtaking prospect across the Goyt Valley).

Now, follow the path through the wood, keeping close to the wall on your right. When you meet the next wall, turn left and again keep this wall on your right, until – finally – you reach Windgather Rocks.

Turn left here and follow the path which soon runs alongside the road, all the way back to your car.

Windgather Rocks

Walks: KR5 and KR6

Route: Lamaload, Forest Chapel, Shutlingsloe (optional), Cat and Fiddle and the Tors.

Starting Point: Car Park, east of Lamaload Reservoir (SJ976753)

Length: 7 miles or 11 miles. Moderate

Duration: 3 hours or 5 hours.

Walking in this area is enhanced by the many fine hills – a fact that would not have been appreciated quite as much by the men and mules taking salt across this rugged area from Northwich to Yorkshire. Saltersford, the name of a local hamlet is derived from this trade; the men leading the mules were called 'salters' (funnily enough) or 'jaggers' (somewhat more obscure). Apart from its association with an ageing pop star, the latter term can still be found in Jagger's Clough, a few miles away.

The paths used on these walks are some of the most well used in the area. Certainly, they are popular, but with good reason – they comprise a classic pair of walks, each starting at Lamaload. Walk KR5 is the shorter one and is ideal for an afternoon stroll. Walk KR6 involves a little more hill climbing, but smashing views to reward you. The first part of each walk, as far as Forest Chapel – is the same, so you can always change your mind about the route to follow when you reach the chapel. Also, to give you a third choice, you can just do the second half of the walk, planning your own link between Forest Chapel and the Cat and Fiddle.

Remember – both walks start at the same place and cover the same ground as far as Forest Chapel, so the first part of the description is the same. ALSO – the final part of the route is the same – only the bits in the middle differ!

Walks KR5 and KR6 – first part of both walks

From the car park (1), go back to the road; turn right and walk along the road (about half a mile) to where it crosses a stream and then begins to climb steeply. Take the first turn right, along a track (2), first crossing a stile adjacent to a gate. Go along the track, until you arrive at a building on your right (remains of Lower

Ballgreave Farm). Turn left off the track here and climb uphill to the remnants of a drystone wall. Turn left here, keeping the wall on your left and head for the next ruined farm (Higher Ballgreave Farm). Keep to the right of the buildings, and then follow the lower (downhill) track.

At a stream (4), go through or over a gate (the stile has long-since gone), and turn right. Go through two more gates and then follow the track which climbs gradually to the left (but not as far over as to the house on your extreme left). Head through some marshy ground to a ruined building on the skyline (5); from here, pause for a moment to look back to Lamaload and the distant moors to the north.

Now continue in the same direction to a gateway; go through this and head to the top right hand corner of the field. The stile here was thoroughly obstructed when first I recommended this walk in early 1987, but after much badgering, the local council tell me that a new stile and footpath sign are being installed. Good News!

Cross the main road, turn right and then immediately left along a short stretch of country lane. At the end, turn left along a road and continue until you reach a track (6) to Greenways Farm. Turn right here, go through the farmyard (behind the house) and cross the new stile in the left-hand corner of the farm yard; this is not quite as shown on the O.S. map, but is very acceptable. Go downhill to a group of hawthorn bushes and cross the stile to the left of them, also crossing a small stream (7).

From here go uphill, and continue straight ahead, crossing a stile, and carrying on to a further clump of hawthorn; the path now continues straight ahead with Shutlingsloe as a distant waymark, eventually passing through another farmyard just before Macclesfield Forest Chapel (8).

This tiny chapel dates back to 1673; a rush-bearing service takes place here (as at nearby Jenkin Chapel). In the case of Forest Chapel, the churchyard is left uncut until the rush-bearing event, which encourages a proliferation of wild flowers. According to a notice in the entrance, around 70 varieties of flowers are found in and around the church yard – including mountain pansies, sweet cicely and poppies; I've spotted some, but not all!

From the chapel, there are two possible routes for you to choose: the short route is described first, the longer one second. BUT PLEASE NOTE – *the final part of each route is the same* and is at the end of this route description headed **Main Route**.

Short Route (KR5)

For the shorter route, turn left along the track from the chapel; at the road (9), turn left again and continue just past the T-junction. Just after the junction, turn right along a tarmac track which crosses a stream. Go through a farmyard and out through a gate to go uphill, with a wall on your left. The next stile is indicated on the O.S. map (10) as being in the top left corner of this field but, in its absence, it's more sensible to use the gate a little to the right.

From the gate, bear left (45 degrees) and cross the field to a ladder stile. Turn right here and keep the wall on your right, crossing a stile, and going straight ahead to a further stile near a derelict building. Cross the stile, go down a flight of stone steps, then turn left to walk between two parallel walls (11). From here, your route lies straight ahead to Torgate Farm. Follow the path through the farm to the road (12), then turn right and walk up the hill; this is a tedious, but unavoidable stretch of road-walking. (It is of interest that the right of way is shown on the O.S. map as heading north-west after Torgate Farm, but everyone uses the farm track, the farmer is happy about it – and it saves an even longer uphill slog for us!)

Turn right at the main road, then left along a track just after the 'Shining Tor' restaurant and cafe. (Could it be time for a tea stop? – the hot chocolate fudge cake is recommended!).

From here, skip the next section and proceed to the **Main Route** at the end of this description to finish your walk.

Longer Route (KR6)

For the longer route, from the Chapel (8), turn right along the road, then first left and proceed to the T-junction (13). Turn right here and walk up this steep road as far as a junction (14). Note that you can avoid some of this road walking by going through the forest (see sketch map) but more open views are enjoyed from the road.

Go straight ahead at the junction, along a concessionary path which eventually leads into the forest and towards the ruins of 'Ferriser'. I'm unsure of the origin of this name – perhaps it was connected with the blacksmith's trade.

Beyond the building and towards the top of the hill, turn left up some steps to a stile – watch out for the steps as they are not too obvious. After just a short distance, the footpath is signposted to "Wildboarclough via Shutlingsloe Farm". The track is very obvious and eroded due to over-walking and under-surfacing. An interesting stile along this route, has for years, involved a precarious balancing act across a bog but, eventually, the track dries out and leads you up to the top of Shutlingsloe (there is also a lower path – see map). Beats me why a heavily-used path like this can't be sorted out to prevent erosion. But thank heaven for small mercies – I'm told that the farmer used to take pot shots at ramblers on Shutlingsloe before the right of way was established!

From the top, bear left and head downhill towards Shutlingsloe Farm. Keep to the right of the farm and go down a tarmac track as far as a cattle grid, where you turn sharp left along a minor track (16) to Bank Top. A path eventually leads down to the road where you climb a ladder stile and either turn left to continue the walk or turn right to make a small diversion: the Crag Inn is temptingly close at this stage, and there's a useful tea shop just south of The Crag, so you're assured of some sort of refreshment at this stage.

Walk along the road (i.e. uphill and away from The Crag) and, just before a large farm, find a stile on your right. Cross this and follow the path which leads to the right of the farm house and then through the farm yard to Clough House car park. Bear right after the farm so that you leave the car park by its easterly exit. Cross the road to a gateway (17), signposted 'Public Footpath to Cat and Fiddle Inn'. Do not be disturbed by the fact that a right of way is not shown on the OS map – this really is correct and is very easy to follow. Cross Cumberland Brook by way of a narrow bridge and continue uphill until you reach a T-junction of paths (18). On your right is a waterfall (in damp weather) but you turn left along a slightly less well worn track. Eventually the path rises sharply, with a small waterfall on your right. You should also note a two foot high stone which serves as a useful marker at the top of this section of the path. From this point, ignore the path on your left – instead, climb the hill straight ahead and cross the gap in a stone wall; then follow a second wall on your right, until you reach a flatter, open area. Continue straight ahead to a T-junction of paths (19). Take a left turn here along an obvious path that takes you to the Cat and Fiddle. On a clear day, the views from this path are unbeatable; the beer's quite good too.

Opening times may have rewarded you; in any event, from the pub, head north (i.e. towards Macclesfield) along the main road, until just past a bend to the left, where you fork right (20) along a well-used track which used to be the main road – spot the milestone with distances to both Macclesfield and London!

The track leads to the Shining Tor cafe. This is point (21) on our map and, from here, we rejoin the *main route*.

Main Route

From a point just to the south of the cafe, follow the track northwards crossing a stile on your right, about 50 yards before Stake Farm (22). Continue straight ahead, crossing one stile, then continuing to a break in the wall, where you turn left and cross a ladder stile (23).

The (almost invariably muddy) path lies straight ahead, with the wall on your left. This part of the walk is the boundary between Cheshire and Derbyshire. Fine views will reward you on a good day; when the thermals are rising, you should see a fair number of hang-gliders on the western slopes of the Tors and, at one particular point, you'll glimpse Errwood Reservoir to the east (your right).

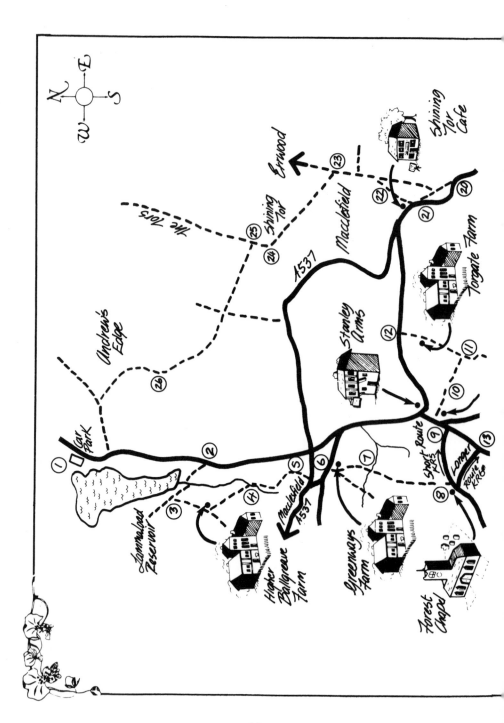

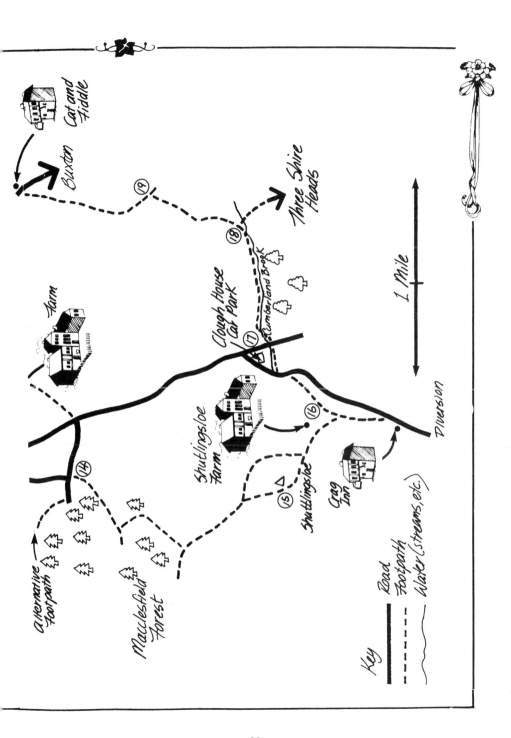

Cat and Fiddle

Buxton

Three Shire Heads

⑲

⑱

Cumberland Brook

Farm

Clough House Car Park

⑰

Shutlingsloe Farm

⑯

⑭

Shutlingsloe

⑮

Crag Inn

Diversion

Alternative Footpath

Macclesfield Forest

1 Mile

Key

Road
Footpath
Water (streams, etc.)

At the top of Shining Tor (24), the trig point on your left denotes the highest point in Cheshire. Having admired it, continue for 100 yards or so to a stile on your left (25), signposted 'Saltersford and Rainow'. Go in this direction, crossing one stile *en-route*.

The path, initially almost due east, bends northwards and gives excellent views of Cats Tor on your right (the name is said to come from the packs of wild cats that inhabited the moors – you may find a better derivation).

Continue along the path until you reach the top of the hill (26), where you'll have a fine view of Lamaload on your left. The path then goes downhill, crossing a rough and ready stile. Continue down the hill, passing the ruins of Eaves Farm on your right. Follow the path further downhill with a small stream and fence on your left, until you meet the road. Turn right here and walk back to the car park at Lamaload Reservoir.

Lamaload – a view from near to the Buxton road with Whaley Moor in the distance

Walk: KR7

Route: Todd Brook Circular: Pym Chair, Dunge Farm, Saltersford.

Starting Point: Pym Chair car park SJ995767, or lay-by down the hill 100 yards to the west.

Length: 7 miles

Duration: 3 hours. Easy/Moderate (except for the walk back to the car park!)

The area between Rainow and Kettleshulme evokes the best of East Cheshire hill country: lonely, sometimes bleak, but with its own rugged beauty and occasional surprises. The last time I did this walk was after a long hard working week; it was early spring, the air was – indeed – like champagne. There's another bonus in starting a walk at Pym Chair – you're often lucky enough to see the radio-controlled gliders that are a popular pastime around here; it always amazes me that they can land their craft just a few feet from the launching point. Mind you, some visitors miss the whole point and *only* watch the gliders.

Parking your car at the lay-by below Pym Chair – i.e. downhill, to the west – is advisable, if there's room: it saves some of the final hard slog on your return journey. But, from whichever starting point, head downhill and westwards until the road levels out, then turn right (1) over two stiles towards Green Stack Farm. Keep to the right of the farm (2) then follow the footpath straight ahead, keeping to the left of the wall. The path crosses a stile to a substantial stone barn. Keep straight on and head down hill; if the somewhat rickety fence is still there, keep to the right of it and, in any event, head towards the clump of trees in front of Dunge Farm.

Before reaching the farm, turn right down a short track (3), and go through a gate to cross stream. Turn left along the track, keeping the lawn of the house on your right. From spring to autumn, the garden here is a fine sight – and a big surprise to walkers who think of Dunge Farm as an unattractive-sounding farmhouse in a bleak area!

Now follow the track to a cattle grid, where you turn left (4) passing a house and stables on your right. Pass through a gate, then turn left and head downhill to a disused building (5). Cross a stile here, then cross a further nearby stile on your left, leading you across a field to cross a stream.

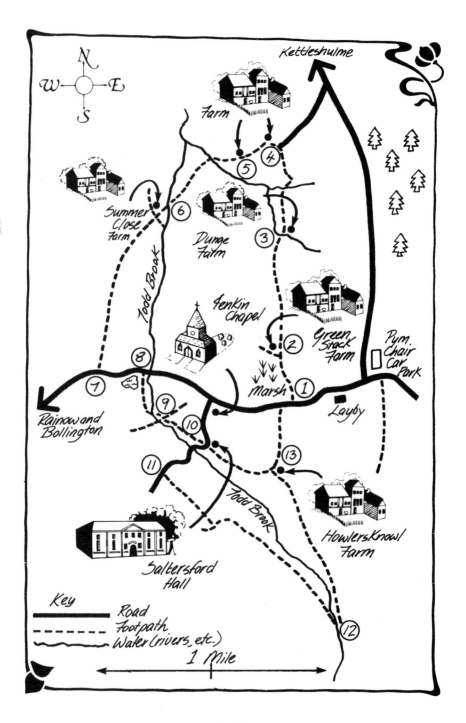

Kettleshulme

Farm

Summer Close Farm

Todd Brook

Dunge Farm

Jenkin Chapel

Green Stack Farm

Pym Chair Car Park

Marsh

Layby

Rainow and Bollington

Todd Brook

Howlers Knowl Farm

Saltersford Hall

Key

Road
Footpath
Water (rivers, etc.)

1 Mile

After this, turn right and find the stile by the gate. Turn left here and follow a row of trees running parallel to a wall on your left. Go through a gate and along a grassy track; as this bends to the left, just before a large holly bush, fork right and cross Todd Brook by a bridge. On the map, the path is shown as passing immediately to the left of the farm (Summer Close), but a diversion takes you 30 yards to the left, joining a farm track via a gate. Turn right at the track and head uphill along a clear – initially sunken – track.

Towards the top of the hill, the path appears to veer left, but just follow the wall on your left. Pause to admire, on your extreme left, Windgather Rocks, which run south to Cats Tor and Shining Tor – the highest point in Cheshire. Continue to a minor lane, where you turn left (7).

At the bottom of the hill, go past the pool belonging to the house on your right, then turn immediately right through a gate (8). Note that this permissive path has been introduced as a far preferable alternative to disturbing the occupants of this pleasant home. It also makes for a more logical route. Having gone through the gate, go straight ahead and find a stile a little to the right and then head towards a stone barn. Cross a stile, then a footbridge (9), following Todd Brook to the road (10).

From here, you have a choice – stay with me, or go via Saltersford Hall Farm straight to Howlers Knowl Farm (13), there rejoining my recommended path. This might be handy if – heaven forbid – the weather turns foul.

For those accompanying me, turn right and head uphill. As the road levels out, turn left (11) along a farm track. Immediately before the farm, go through a gateway and turn left, keeping the wall on your left. Cross two stiles (the first of which was very neglected in 1987) and head for the top left corner of the field. Cross a stile here and go straight ahead, following the contour of the hill.

Where the path meets the junction of three old walls, begin to head downhill, crossing a stile just above a stream. Continue in the same direction, keeping well to the right of the more prominent stream – Todd Brook again! Eventually, the path becomes fairly obvious – cross an old wall and a stile which leads to a track crossing Todd Brook (12). If in full flood, it is easier to cross a little further upstream.

Follow the path until you reach a ruined building: turn left and follow the track northwards. This path continues straight ahead, keeping a constant height. Eventually, it heads downhill towards Howlers Knowl farm (13) which is linked by a path from Saltersford Hall Farm. Walk along the farm drive to the road, where you turn right and return – up a hill that seems steeper than when you came down it just 3 hours ago – to your car.

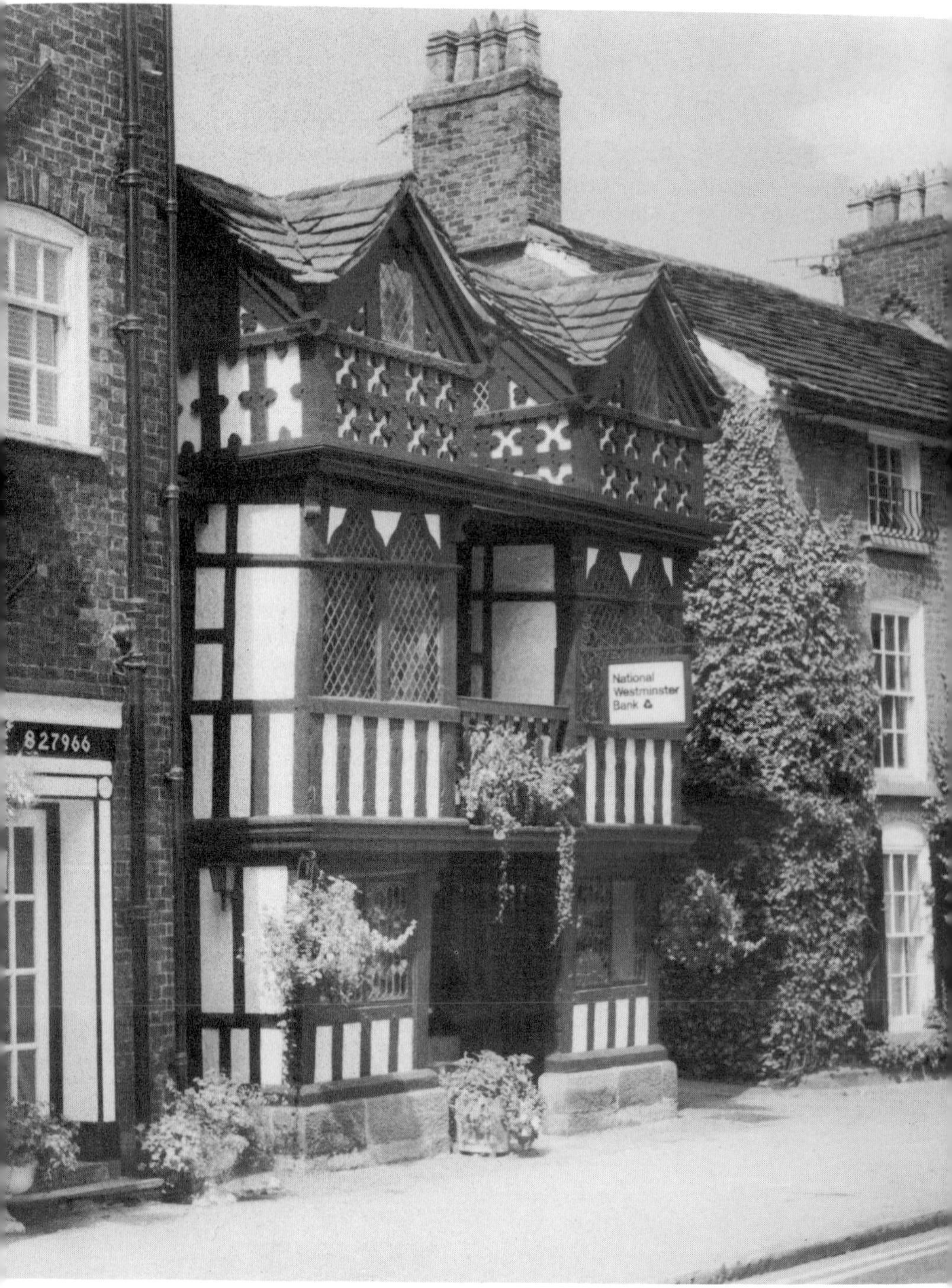

827966
National
Westminster
Bank

The Prestbury Area

Prestbury has two faces. To many people, it is the quaint, rather twee, main street with up-market shops and an inevitable upper-crust image. But, also, it is an historic village of great charm, lying in some of the most beautiful Cheshire countryside. To me, it has the perfect combination for walking: some hills to make the walk worthwhile, but a lush greenness so often lacking in the wilder areas further East.

About the Village

The village takes its name from the Saxon *Preost burgh*, or Priest's Town. The first settlement was made around 670 A.D. by missionary priests. In fact, one of our walks begins in Priest Lane, just to emphasise the monastic influence. St. Peter's Church is the most notable building in the village, with a Norman chapel nearby on the South-east side. A further priestly connection is the 15th century Priest's House, a black and white building in the village centre, now the National Westminster bank. Seemingly, the vicar once addressed his parishioners from the balcony on this building during the Commonwealth, when the church was closed to him by the Puritans.

Like many villages in Cheshire, Prestbury later became associated with the weaving industry. In Prestbury's case, it was silk, as it was on a much larger scale in nearby Macclesfield. The silk merchants used to drive their wagons across the Bollin, which flows through Prestbury, by way of a ford. This is still remembered today in the name of Ford House which is near to the bridge built by the profits of the silk trade. But for a local benefactor, Ford House almost became a gambling casino!

That is as much as we can say about the village itself in this short space. The parish of Prestbury is, surprisingly, one of the largest in England. Next time you are driving around this area, just see how far the Prestbury boundary signs extend. Even Tytherington, which most people think of as being in Macclesfield, is part of the parish of Prestbury.

The Walks

The footpath routes around Prestbury are such that it is difficult to work out more than three or four decent circular walks which begin in Prestbury village. Also, some paths end on busy main roads, necessitating lengthy road walking. The walks to be described are, I hope, a good selection for this highly attractive area.

Walk: P1

Route: Mottram Cross to Adder's Moss

Starting Point: Priest Lane (below the Bull's Head on Mottram-Prestbury road) SJ880785

Length: Three miles. Easy.

Duration: One and a quarter hours.

This short walk does not strictly begin in Prestbury, but who's worried? It's nearer to Prestbury than any other major centre, and is a nice, short introduction to the characteristics of the surrounding countryside. Unlike the flatter lands to the East (covering Wilmslow, Mobberley and so on), the countryside in the Prestbury and Mottram areas is just hilly enough to be interesting without exhausting–almost as though the fields have been tipped up for you to admire.

In Priest Lane, convenient parking spots are either about 200 yards down the lane, just past the entrance to Brook House farm, or a little further down, at the start of our walk, opposite Priest Cottage. (Take care not to block the field gate).

Go over the stile opposite Priest Cottage, (1), along a track, and turn right at the end of it, heading uphill. Continue straight ahead to the road, climbing one stile en route. The stile to the road is in the far corner of the field, beside a house (2).

Turn left at the road, walk past Goose Green Farm on your right and after about a quarter of a mile turn right (3) at the gate opposite to a farm on your left, into a field.

The path crosses this field to a stile; head straight across the next field just to the right of a wood (Alder Wood). The path dips down to some iron railings, (looking as though they will soon be replaced) which you go through.

Walk around Alder Wood (4), until a larger wood (Daniel Hill Wood) is on your right. The path now heads parallel to Daniel Hill Wood (about 100 yards to your right) along a well-worn field track, through Mount Farm to the road. (Most of the track is invariably very muddy–so be prepared.)

Note: a new National Trust path now passes *through* Alder Wood, parallel to the path suggested. The path through the wood used to be virtually impassable.

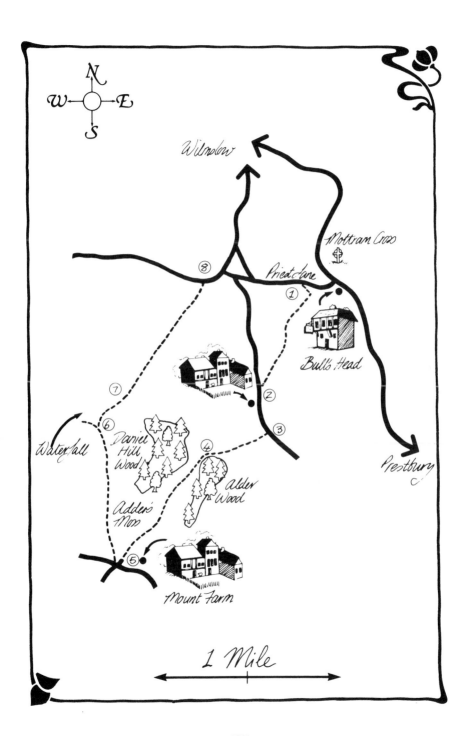

Wilmslow

Mottram Cross

Priest Lane

⑧

①

Bull's Head

②

③

⑦

Waterfall

⑥

Daniel Hill Wood

④

Alder Wood

Adder's Moss

⑤

Mount Farm

Prestbury

N
W E
S

1 Mile

Turn right at the road then right again (5) along another road, quickly degenerating into a track. Bear to the right at Adder's Moss Farm, and continue along the track which passes below Hill Top Farm on your far right. Further to your right, there are fine views of the hill ranges of the Peak District.

Where the farm drive turns right, cross the stile facing you, into the field. Halfway along the hedge (on your left) there is a stile (6) – climb over this for a small diversion from our walk. Go down the path to Waterfall Wood, follow the sound of running water and you'll see how the wood got its name. Now, back to the stile, turn left and continue walking along the edge of the field, to a stile in its top left corner.

Climb this stile, then immediately another one, and turn left. After about ten yards, the path heads precipitously downhill (7) from the main path, through the wood, joining a wide well-defined track.

Follow the track then continue along the footpath into a field with the hedge on your left. In the far left corner of the field, cross first one footbridge, then another, and continue through the next and final field to the road (8) where you turn right.

At the road junction, turn right at Priest Lane and head back to where you started.

The View to Alder Wood

Walk: P2

Route: Prestbury to Mottram

Starting Point: Main car park in Prestbury (behind the Admiral Rodney); SJ902773

Length: Six miles. Easy/Moderate.

Duration: Two and a half hours.

This is a walk that never strays far away from the River Bollin, and benefits from the excellent Bollin Valley Project – waymarking, decent stiles, and little chance of getting lost. Even so, I confess that I lost my way once on this walk, simply by believing that the waymarks would be so obvious that a map was not necessary; I was wrong!

Walk North through the car park past the bungalows. Turn left along Scott Road into Bollin Grove, after which a track leads to the River Bollin. Turn right here, (signposted Wilmslow), going alongside the Bollin (also by the Sewage Works, so keep moving!).

After the Sewage Works, the waymarked path continues through the fields. On reaching a bridge, head for the top right hand corner of the field you are in, climb the stile, and follow the waymark towards the left of the farm ("Top o'th' Hill") facing you. The path goes through the farmyard, by way of a stile and then, after the farm, turn left over a stile, and along a path that runs parallel to the road on your right. Eventually the path switches to the left hand side of the hedge, and continues to the main road (2).

Turn left at the road, then go over the stile (signposted Mill Lane) to the right of a drive. The path heads slightly to the right and goes through a series of stiles (be sure to cross each one you encounter, as two of them switch you over to the other side of the hedge). All beautifully waymarked, all the way to Mottram Bridge, on Mill Lane (3).

Cross the bridge, then turn left to walk along the waymarked path, which heads between a cottage and Mill Farm and generally upstream towards Mottram Hall Hotel along a waymarked path.

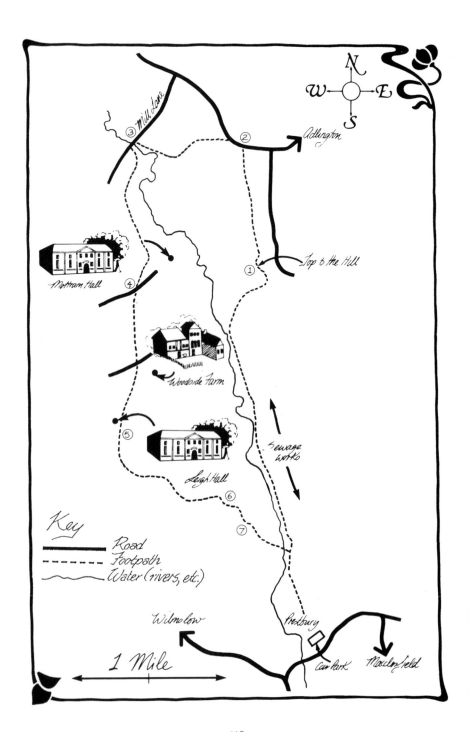

N
W E
S

Mill Lane
③

② Adlington

① Top o' the Hill

Mottram Hall
④

Woodside Farm

Leigh Hall
⑤

⑥

⑦

Sewage works

Key
Road
Footpath
Water (rivers, etc.)

Wilmslow

Prestbury
Car Park
Macclesfield

1 Mile

The path that we want bends to the right, a hundred yards or so before the hotel and crosses the hotel drive, by way of two iron gates (4).

From here, walk straight ahead, towards a farm, heading just to the right of it. The path crosses the drive to the farm, and heads up through the fields to Legh Hall; note that the path starts on the right of the hedge but, after 100 yards, crosses to the left at a stile. Walk along the walled drive to Legh Hall (5), then turn left along a track (signposted "Prestbury"). The route from here is waymarked, but a few notes may help you.

After leaving the outbuildings of Legh Hall, a "kissing gate" takes you into a field. Turn right here and follow the hedge to a stile at the far left hand corner of the field. Continue along the edge of the next field, cross another stile and carry on towards the right of the farm facing you. The path crosses the farm track and goes to the right and behind the farm buildings.

At the next stile, where there is no waymark sign, turn right and walk to the right of the barn to another stile, which *is* waymarked!

Turn left here and follow the fence to another stile which you cross and turn right.

From here, the rest of the path is obvious. It drops down, through two further stiles, to a footbridge (7), then round to the right and over another stile. Notice that a house and outbuilding should now be behind you – the natural and wrong inclination is to head toward them and there is no waymark to help you.

From here, turn left and follow the hedge, passing through a stile in the bottom left hand corner of the field, with the house on your left. Then, turn left to a stile on the drive to the house, where you turn right.

Finally, follow the drive down to the River Bollin, turn right, and head for home.

Walk: P3

Route: Prestbury to Whiteley Green

Starting Point: Main car park in Prestbury (behind the Admiral Rodney); SJ902773

Length: Four and a half miles. Easy/Moderate

Duration: Two hours.

This is a varied walk, including some gentle hills which give good views of "real" hills just a few miles away. You'll also walk along the old road from Butley Town towards Bollington – now, scarcely a cart track.

Walk out of the car park towards Prestbury (i.e. the way you drove in) and turn right along the main road. Then turn left into Bridge Green and after about 100 yards, head to the right along a grassy track signposted "Macclesfield"(1). You will find the first part of the walk to be well waymarked.

The path crosses a stream and then keeps to the right. Follow the line of the stream, and then a waymarked path until you come to a stile. Turn right here, and soon afterwards, left at the next stile. From here, the scenery begins to unfold, with Prestbury on your right, and the hills behind Bollington on your left. As you walk along this path, Kerridge Hill is slightly to your left, with White Nancy sitting on Kerridge's left-most "knee".

You are now on a golf course and the safest path is to follow the perimeter fence on your left. Alternatively, you can follow the definitive (and slightly longer) path along a line of trees until, near the 12th and 15th tees (about 300 yards before a stream), you turn left along the newly diverted path towards the perimeter fence. When you reach it, turn right. Whichever route you choose, the path passes between two parallel fences to a stile, where you turn left and follow the path to Heybridge Lane.

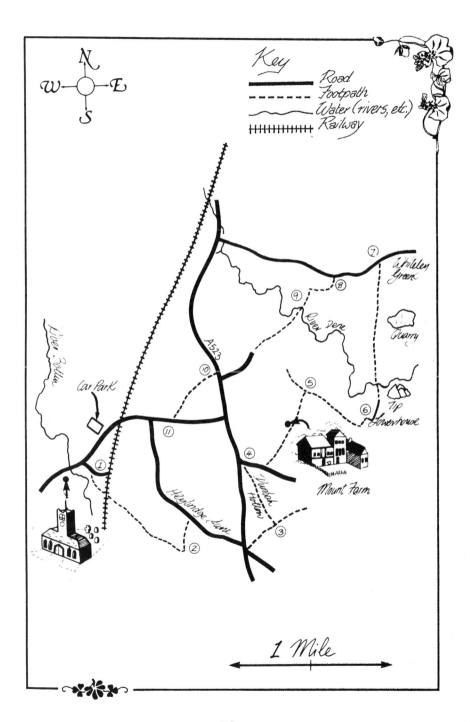

Cross this busy road with care, turn right, then first left at the footpath sign, up the drive to "Dumbah". After passing the large house on your right, the path heads down hill. Just before the next house, turn left at a stile (3) and cross straight over the field. Now follow the stiles in a straight line through Dumbah Hollow – an attractive and popular little walking area. The stile at the end of Dumbah Hollow is on the right hand side – to the right of an ivy covered house. The path goes over a small bridge, and crosses a field to the Bollington Road (4).

Turn right here, then after 100 yards, turn left and walk along the drive to Mount Farm. Walk past the farm keeping it on your right (there is an alternative path through the farm, but there's little advantage in using it). The well made drive degenerates into a rough track. After about 150 yards, turn right (5) – keeping the fence on your right. Notice that there is also a stile to the left, taking you along a path to Butley Town. This path, from Butley in the direction of Bollington, was the old road to Bollington – long before Prestbury assumed its present importance.

So, carry on along this path towards Bollington – you'll see White Nancy straight ahead.

About half way along this path, where there is a stile in the fence on your right, turn *left* towards a wooded area bordering a river. Turn right here and follow the river upstream – this path has miraculously changed since my disparaging comments about it in the first edition of this book! After crossing a stile, the path bears right, crosses a field and heads towards a stile, opposite to a large factory building. Turn left here and follow a track in the direction of the household waste site.

Just before the Household Waste Tip, there is a stile on your left. Pass through the stile, and carry on in a straight line for almost a mile, until you reach the road at Whiteley Green (7). *Note:* Ignore the road to Whiteley Green Quarry; the stile onto the road is just to the left of the farm.

Turn left at the stile, and walk down the road for a quarter of a mile. Just after the road bends to the right, you go straight ahead and through or over a gate (8) on your left (about 30 yards after the quarry entrance).

Follow the hedge, passing under the electricity cables, then sharply left and across a footbridge over the River Dene (9).

From here, the path heads slightly to the right to a stile in the top right hand corner of the field, some 50 yards to the right of a gate. Follow the hedge (on your right) and you will eventually walk through the farmyard and onto a minor road, which leads back to the main (A523) road.

Cross the road, turn right, then first left across a stile to the right of the farm entrance (10). This rejoins the Bollin Valley Project so you will find it to be well waymarked – start off by keeping to the hedge (on your left). After the footbridge, turn slightly left and head for a white bungalow (11) – the stile is nearly opposite it.

Finally turn right and head back to Prestbury.

Prestbury Village.

Walk: P4

Route: Withinlee Road, the Golf Course and Big Wood.

Starting Point: SJ883769 (Withinlee Road, half a mile from its junction with the main Prestbury to Wilmslow Road).

Length: Three and a half miles. Easy/Moderate.

Duration: One and a half hours.

Park on Withinlee Road, near the footpath sign on your left: walk back along this road, and turn right at the main road. After about a quarter of a mile, turn right into Castle Gate (2). Just as this road swings to the left, turn into Castleford Drive, immediately turn left and walk down a footpath between two tall hedges – that's got the road walking out of the way!

This path leads directly to a road, where you turn left and join Chelford Road (3).

Turn right here then, after fifty yards, left into the golf course. This path runs alongside a hedge, down to Spencer Brook. From the brook, the path lies straight ahead. Follow the marker posts along this easy path – noting that it swings to the right in front of a small wood, afterwards passing along a track between a wooden fence and a hedge.

At the Golf Club drive (4), turn right, then turn left at a small flight of stone steps. This leads to a clearly defined and waymarked path, emerging at a minor service road with "Pennsylvania" (5) on your right.

Cross the road to a stile to the next public footpath (the notice posted by The Kings School does not affect access, nor is it meant to). The path follows the perimeter of the playing field until it reaches three stone steps on your right. Cross these and turn left. Follow the edge of this field, then turn left at the gate and head towards the farm (6).

Before you reach the farm house, turn right at a stone wall. Walk alongside this, then turn right into the next field. Walk alongside the fence, and cross the stile in the corner. Carry on in the same direction that you were walking, until you come to a pair of stone gate posts. Go through these (or over the nearby stile) and carry on with the fence on your left.

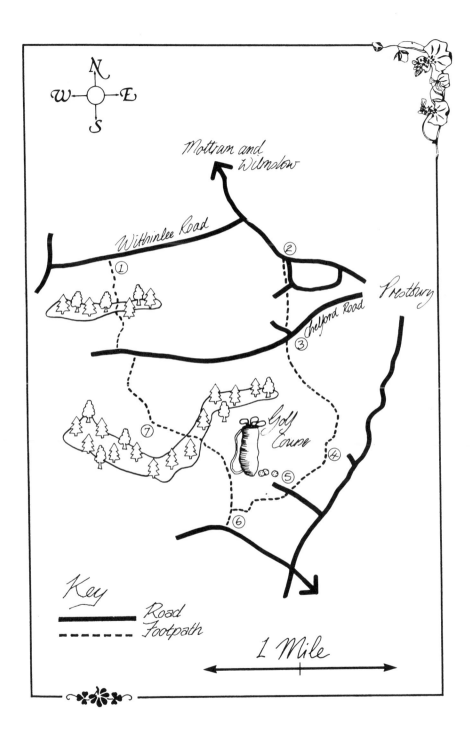

Turn left at the next stile and cross a further stile. Continue with the fence on your left towards a wood. As you reach the wood, turn right and then cross the stile into the wood on your left. A footbridge crosses the stream, taking you to a path leading uphill and out of the wood.

Cross the next stile and go straight ahead, with the hedge on your right.

In the top-right corner of the field (7) cross a stile, then almost immediately turn left over an old stile (rather easier to walk over the derelict adjacent gate on my last visit) and follow the old hedge that is facing you. Your next stile is a few yards to the right of a gate which, in turn, is almost in the top right corner of the field.

Cross the stile (and stream) and walk uphill with the hedge on your left. Be sure to look over your shoulder at the top of the hill – there is a splendid view, right over to the Peak District hills.

Turn left at the road, then right after about 80 yards along the path to Crabtree Cottage. Just before the gate to the house, turn right through a wooden gate and follow the waymarked path through the wood and back to where you started from.

The Norman Chapel, Prestbury (photo: John Creighton)

Siddington and
The Peovers

Like many of the Western areas covered in this book, Siddington and the various Peovers lie in rich dairy-farming and arable country.

Siddington is a sprawling parish with no real village centre. Its name derives from that of the de Sydington family who settled here in the time of Henry III. The most notable place to visit in the area is Capesthorne Hall, home of the Bromley-Davenport family. Apart from the usual attractions of a stately home, there is a nature trail through the park which will keep the children busy.

The Peovers comprise Higher Peover, Lower Peover and Peover Heath. You'll scarcely know where one finished and the next begins and you may become even more puzzled by the alternative names of Peover Superior, Peover Inferior and Nether Peover. But, it is well worth persevering. Peover Hall, in Higher Peover, was due for demolition, but it is now restored and is open to the public occasionally. It is accessed along a private drive leading from Grotto Lane which also leads to St. Lawrence's, often referred to as Cheshire's Hidden Church.

Lower Peover's greatest claims to fame are the Bells of Peover Inn, and the almost adjacent St. Oswald's Church. This contains a chest said to be carved from a single piece of oak. The lid is so heavy that it was used to assess the strength of any girl intending to wed a local farmer – obviously you needed a strong arm as well as a pretty face in those days.

The Walks

The walking around here is all of an easy nature. Not surprisingly, many of the footpaths are also farm drives so you'll see more than the usual amount of agriculture in this section of the book.

Route: Redesmere, Siddington and Capesthorne

Starting Point: Car park adjacent to Redesmere, off the A34 (SJ849713)

Length: Seven miles. Easy.

Duration: Two and a half hours.

This is an easy walk, mainly through some of the farmland and farms of Cheshire – in fact, it is surprising just how many of the public rights of way in this area are farm drives.

I've suggested a clockwise route for this walk – as with most others – because on this particular one we save the lakes of Capesthorne Hall until last – perhaps a good place to stop for a picnic tea. But first, the walk.

Leave your car at the car park alongside Redesmere Lake, which is approached from the A34 along Fanshawe Lane.

Continue along this lane, past Hills Green Farm on your right, then turn right at the stile alongside Fanshawe Brook (1).

Climb the small incline and head through a line of stiles across the fields towards Hazelwall Farm (2). Cross the final fence before the farm by way of a stile and continue to the farm drive, where you turn right.

Cross the main road and walk along Henshaw Lane until the main surface peters out and you reach a fork. Follow the right fork to Henshaw Hall Farm. Pass through the farmyard and follow the track which leads through Heskey Wood (the first wood you pass through), then forks left (3) past Moss Wood. The path now heads towards a farm; as your route passes the end of Moss Wood, turn left and follow a path between two hedges to the farm. Struggle over a gate, pass through the farmyard and walk along the farm drive.

Turn right at the road; continue for about a quarter of a mile and turn right onto a track (4) which runs along the right hand edge of a field, until you reach a stile. Turn right here and continue along a track to the right of a wood, then through Northwood Farm, Sandbank Farm and back to the A34.

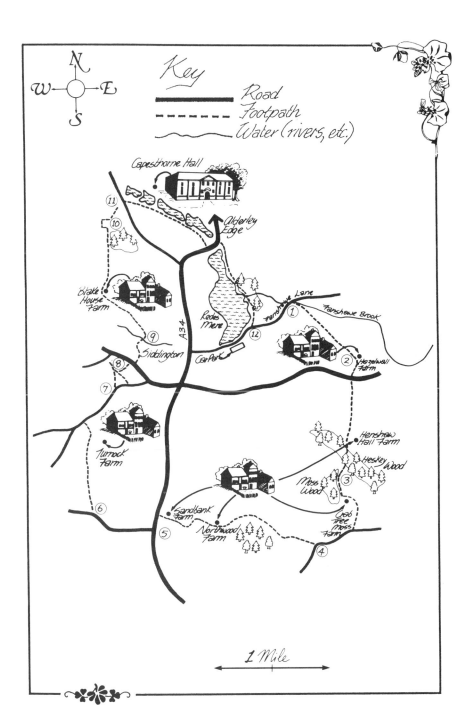

Turn left here, then right along Blackden Lane (5) to the first farm drive on your right (6), signposted to Siddington. Continue straight ahead across a series of stiles until you arrive at the drive to Turnock Farm (the path joins the drive midway between Turnock Farm on your right and the house on your left). Turn left here and continue to the main road, where you turn right and continue until Dickory Cottage (7), which is on your left.

Fork left, along a grassy track. Before you reach the next road (if you have done, turn back!), take a hairpin turn to the right (8) in front of two gateways. Follow this path a short distance, then turn left – leading you past a wood on your right.

After crossing the road the footpath is shown on the O.S. map as being straight ahead, along a track which leads behind a group of houses. But, since this will cause you to walk through the backyard of the last house, you may prefer to turn right at the road and take the first turn left, to walk along the road in *front* of the houses.

Keep to the left, passing in front of a group of bungalows, then head along a path into a wood. About 50 yards after crossing a stream, turn left (9) along a path bounded by two hedges, eventually passing a superb thatched cottage and heading for Blake House Farm.

Turn right at the farm drive and follow it through the farmyard. Continue in the same direction, following a track which leads into a field with a fence on your right and a wood straight ahead.

Cross this field, heading towards its top left hand corner. Enter the next field through a gateway and leave it through the opposite gateway. Now, turn right and follow the edge of the field until you arrive at a stile in a corner of this irregularly shaped field (10). Cross this stile, then the one adjacent to the gate facing you, which leads immediately to yet another stile after crossing a track.

Cross this field, aiming for the top-left corner. Cross over a minor road (11) and enter a field by way of the gate to the right of a small bungalow. Keep to the left and continue past the lakes of Capesthorne Hall – the highlight of the walk! You pass each lake and, finally, a wood on your left until you arrive at the A34.

Turn left here, then right at the gate toward Redesmere. Follow the path around the lake back to your car (12).

Walk: S P2

Route: Over Peover Hall to Lower Peover

Starting Point: Private drive to Over Peover Hall (SJ781733)

Length: Eight miles. Easy.

Duration: Three hours.

This is another of the flat walking areas which, although I prefer the hills, I felt should not be neglected. Many of the paths in this area are well-used, but others are falling into disuse, partly due to the pressures of modern agricultural practices in this lush farming area.

Even though you may prefer the hills, there is plenty to see around here, a fact that is particularly helpful if you are planning a family walk.

Park on the roadside (1) near the drive to Over Peover Church and Hall.

Walk along the drive until you reach the church – note that there is limited parking around the church, but the road is a private one – that's why we've parked where we have!

Take a look around the church, parts of which date back to the 14th Century. One of its claims to fame is that General Patton had his wartime HQ in nearby Peover Hall and worshipped regularly at the church. The hall, by the way, is only open on Mondays in the Summer.

From the church follow the path between two lines of well-manicured beech trees and through the rhododendrons and mature trees of the Peover Estate.

Cross a stile, turn left and then right at the next stile (2). Now, just keep the fence on your right until you reach a stile almost at the end of the field. Cross this and continue in the same direction, joining a track leading directly to Stocks Lane (and the nearby Whipping Stocks pub, with its amazing children's playground).

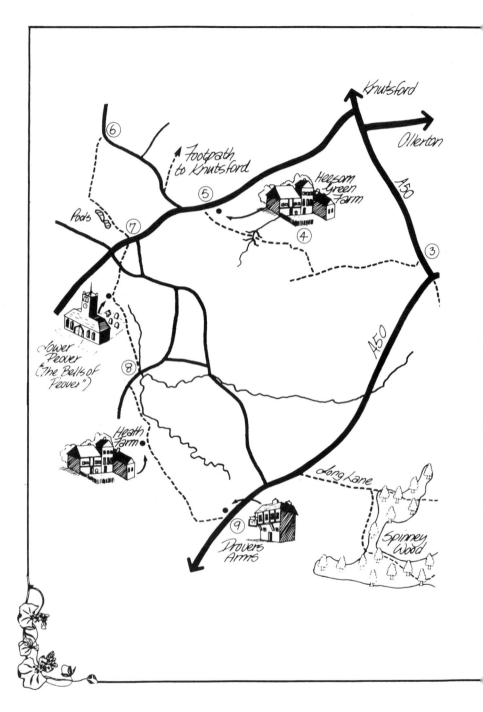

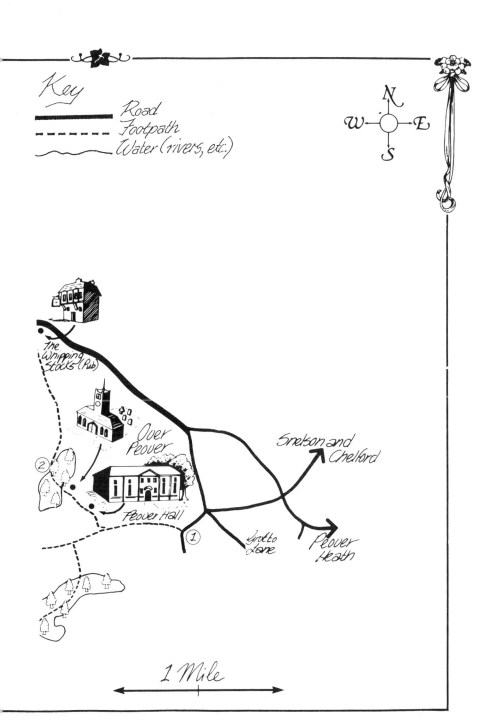

Key

Road
Footpath
Water (rivers, etc.)

The Whipping Stocks (Pub)

Over Peover

Peover Hall

Snelson and Chelford

Grotto Lane

Peover Heath

①

②

1 Mile

Cross the road and follow the A50 in the Knutsford direction, then take the first turn left (3) along a farm road. Ignore the first right fork, go past Sandy Lane Farm on your left, then take the first turn right and pass to the left of some derelict farm buildings (4).

Cross the stile you see ahead of you, and follow the field boundary, leaving by the first gate. Turn left at the next stile and keep the hedge on your left. After the next stile, cross directly over the field to a rickety old footbridge (doubtless by now a magnificent new construction).

Cross this at your peril, go through the gate (or over it – it was securely tied up on my last visit) and then cross the next field, aiming for the mid-point of the opposite hedge.

Climb over the old gate at this point and follow the fence. The path passes a small pool (possibly empty in a dry Summer) and goes through the farmyard to the road (5).

Turn left here, then right along the first lane you come to. Continue past Plumley Lane Farm (noting that you can, if you wish, extend your walk by way of the footpath towards Knutsford which runs behind this farm). Some quarter of a mile later, turn left across a stile (6) as the road bears right.

Walk all around the edge of the field – noting that the right of way actually "cuts the corner" some 50 yards past a hedge in the field on your right, but this has been forgotten due to the conversion of two fields into one mini-prairie.

Cross the stile in the top-left hand corner of the field and follow the track towards the road.

Just before the road (7), bear right, cross the road and then the stile facing you. Turn left after the next stile, then right along a narrow lane leading directly to the church at Lower Peover. Go through the churchyard gate and follow the path to the left of the church.

After leaving the church, turn left along a track which then bends to the right, heading for a wooded area and the river. Follow the river upstream until you meet the road (8), where you turn right, then left through a gateway opposite the large house. Follow the track down to the oddly-called Peover Eye river (which most people seem to reach by the more direct route of crossing at point (8) to a path beside the river), then follow the river and cross two more stiles.

The path now leads uphill, turning left before the outbuildings of Heath Farm to follow the field boundary on your right. After the fourth stile, cross the next field and head for its top right hand corner, essentially carrying on in a straight line. Go through the gateway and turn left towards the Drovers' Arms (9) – another pub with a good children's playground.

Turn left and walk past (or through!) the pub along the A50 until you reach Long Lane on your right.

Walk along here back towards Peover Hall and your starting point. For a scenic diversion, turn right after about 500 yards along Long Lane to pass through Spinney Wood; the path re-joins Long Lane a few hundred yards further along.

Over Peover Church.

Brookside Café, Wildboarclough

Wildboarclough

This is one of the most popular places to visit in East Cheshire. It gives easy access to a large area of surrounding hills and dales, though many visitors never stray far away from the Crag Inn, so it is rarely crowded. Currently, there is some debate as to whether this may change since there are plans to build large car parks and to "develop" the area. I confess to having mixed feelings about this.

Historically, the name is derived from the supposedly last wild boar in England. Whether or not this is true, Wildboarclough was a surprisingly busy place when weaving was in its heyday. The old post office building was part of Crag Mill, an 18th Century silk mill built in the grand Georgian style. There were several other busy mills, including nearby Gradbach Mill which manufactured flax and silk fabrics; nowadays, this mill has been lovingly restored as a youth hostel.

Another interesting area is the nearby Three Shire Heads (often called, incorrectly, Three Shires Head) which is at the junction of Cheshire, Staffordshire and Derbyshire. Way back in the 14th Century, Macclesfield Forest extended to here and local felons used to cross the border to make their getaway, after trapping animals in the forest. More recently, bare-knuckle boxing matches were held here illegally. As, say, the Cheshire constabulary arrived, boxers and spectators would just step over the boundary into, Derbyshire or Staffordshire.

The Walks

This is rugged walking country. You can easily leave the crowds behind to get into unspoilt upland areas belonging to the Peak National Park. Definitely my sort of walking!

Walk: WB1

Route: Wildboarclough, Gradbach and Three Shire Heads.

Starting Point: Old quarry car park 200 yards North of the Crag Inn (SJ983688)

Length: Six and a half miles. Moderate.

Duration: Two and a half hours.

I well remember the last time I walked this route. The weather was abysmal – starting with driving snow and slush underfoot. Unfortunately, the slush was also "under tyre", with the result that my car had a minor argument with a stone wall – walking can be such an expensive hobby! I still enjoyed the walk, and it's even better on a fine day. Gradbach is a pretty place to visit, while Three Shire Heads is ruggedly impressive and a very popular tourist spot – so, try to avoid summer weekends!

Head from the car park downhill, then turn left over the bridge. Take a right turn along a track (1) just after a telephone box on your left.

The path continues straight ahead after passing a garage belonging to the house on your left. Cross the stile and continue through the field to the top left hand corner, where you walk between two stone walls. Then, turn right at the corner of the wall on your right and aim for the top left hand corner of the next field. From here, follow the obvious track between a pair of stone walls.

At the end of this track (also at the farthest reach of the wood), turn left over a stone stile and go straight ahead, towards the next wood (2).

Keep the wood on your right then, as you cross the second tumbledown wall, head for a stone-built building straight ahead. Walk through the farmyard of this old farm (now disused) and follow the track towards the road (3). Note that it bends to the right after about 100 yards heading towards a stile some 20 yards to the left of a gate.

Cross the road, and cross the stile almost opposite, leading upwards to a surfaced track leading round the hill. At the fork in this track, keep left and follow the track all the way to the road.

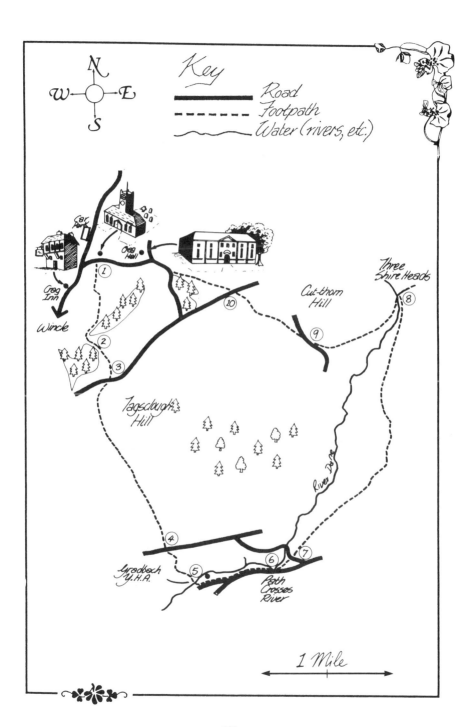

Key

Road
Footpath
Water (rivers, etc.)

Crag Inn

Winde

Crag Hall

Three Shire Heads

Cut-thorn Hill

Tagsclough Hill

River Dane

Gradbach Y.H.A.

Path Crosses River

1 Mile

Cross the road (4) and follow the farm track as far as its sharp bend to the right, where you continue straight ahead, over a stile. Head downhill with the wall on your right, then turn left when you reach the wall facing you.

Cross the first stile on your right and fork slightly left to join a track leading downhill to Gradbach Youth Hostel (5).

From the hostel, follow the road to the left.

After leaving the drive from the hostel, walk straight ahead along a minor road. Just after a passing place for cars (on your right) cross the stile on your left and follow the path alongside the road.

Cross the footbridge (6) then follow the path alongside the River Dane on your left. Leave the field by a stile adjacent to a gateway and turn right.

Walk along the road for some 70 yards, then turn left (7) through a gateway. After entering the field, fork right. Cross the wall at the stile, with the luxury of a signpost.

The path leads straight ahead – you fork slightly to the right leaving the old building on your left and entering the next field through a gateway. From here, carry on straight ahead, with the wall on your left.

When you reach the very end of the wall, continue in the same direction over two stiles. After the second stile, head for the top left hand corner of the field. Go through a stile, then follow the wall on your left. Cross a stile into the next field then walk uphill and to the left of the building facing you. Where the path joins a farm track, walled on either side, turn left and continue straight ahead – ignore any footpath signs, you just follow the main track until you reach the bridges at Three Shire Heads (8). Cross both bridges and continue along the track until you reach the road (Note: the area around Three Shire Heads is well worth exploring – refer to the O.S. map for the area).

Cross the road (9), then immediately go over a stile to the right of a house and follow the path. Initially this runs alongside the wall, then gently forks right to continue straight ahead, across open moorland. Eventually, the path crosses a stile set in a stone wall – some 30 yards to the right of where the wall crumbles into oblivion. Shutlingsloe is a beautiful sight ahead of you.

The path now forks very slightly to the right and leads to the road – you'll see the footpath sign quite soon.

Cross the main road (10) and then the stile facing you. Continue along quite a clear path, again towards Shutlingsloe.

Where the path meets the road, turn right then follow the road downhill, past the church and back to the car park.

Walk: WB2

Route: Wildboarclough, Shutlingsloe and Langley.

Starting Point: Old quarry car park 200 yards North of the Crag Inn (SJ983688)

Length: Seven miles. Moderate/Strenous.

Duration: Three hours.

To be honest, the only strenuous part of the walk is Shutlingsloe – perhaps *the* most prominent hill that you'll see from almost every walk in this book. Be sure to take an O.S. map with you and try to pick out the geographical features. Be warned, however: Shutlingsloe is amazingly popular and you'll rarely be up there alone, so perhaps a weekday visit would be more civilised!

From the car park head downhill, following the Wincle sign. Then, turn sharp right (1) up a private road (also a public path). As you pass the private drive to Bank Top, Shutlingsloe becomes dramatically visible – and quite a different flat-topped shape from its sharp pointed appearance that we take for granted when looking at it from the North.

At the last wall before Shutlingsloe Farm, turn left and follow the waymarked path to the summit.

From the triangulation point on the summit, turn right – you should see a very obvious track below you – this is the one you need. If you have a compass, note that you will be heading almost due North. Where the path meets a second one from the right, you turn left (2) over a plank bridge, following the sign to Langley. Eventually, you reach the outskirts of Macclesfield Forest. Cross the stile (3) into the forest and turn immediately left. This path leads through the forest all the way down to Trentabank Reservoir.

Turn left at the road (4), and follow it to a T-junction, where you turn left. (For an alternative route, see the note at end of this walk.)

Follow the minor road for about one and a half miles. At the T-junction (5), turn left and follow this road as far as The Hanging Gate Inn (6), where you turn left over a stile.

133

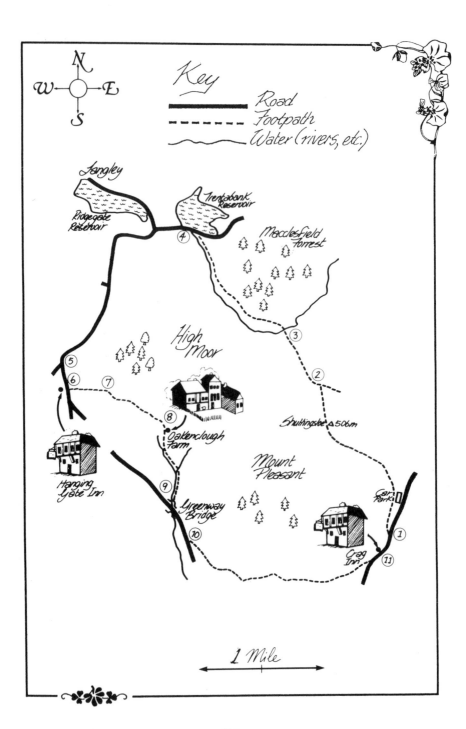

Walk along the track (often waterlogged) until you reach another stile. Turn right here (7), then left at the wall, keeping the wall on your left. At the end of the wall, continue along the path, passing a small pond. As the path goes over the hill, you'll see Oakenclough, a large farm, ahead of you.

Head straight towards the farm (8) following the waymark signs. The footpath leads through a gate just before the main building, and runs alongside the wall on your left. After crossing two stiles, carry on downhill to join the path on the left of the stream. Follow this waymarked path downhill to the road, where you turn left (9).

Continue along the road and then fork left along a farm track (10). Where the track bends sharply to the left, leave the track and cross a stile on your right. Go through a gate then fork right heading between the second and third power-line poles from the left, aiming for a clear gap in the wall, though that is not your destination.

The path crosses a stream then forks right towards a stile at the right hand end of a stone wall on your right.

Continue straight ahead through a series of waymarked stiles. Eventually, the Crag Inn comes into view and the path drops down to a stile (11). Turn left after crossing this and return to the car.

Note: if you object to the stretch of road-walking from Trentabank Reservoir, follow the road to the North side of Ridgegate Reservoir and pick up the Gritstone Trail, going due South. You'll definitely need an O.S. map to connect up with point number (5) on the map, but it's a worthwhile if somewhat lengthier exercise.

Shutlingsloe (the high peak in the distance)

Walk: WB3

Route: The Cat and Fiddle, Errwood and Burbage Edge.

Starting Point: Layby near the Cat and Fiddle Inn, on the A537. (SK001719)

Length: Eight and a half miles. Moderate/Strenuous.

Duration: Three hours.

This walk, being in a book of "East Cheshire Walks" may seem like a bit of a cheat: although it begins in Cheshire, ninety percent of it is in Derbyshire! However, my defence is that it would be a shame not to include a walk in the Goyt Valley: an area that can be ruggedly icy in the Winter, but a paradise in Spring and Summer, if you don't mind meeting many more walkers!

Parking is easy – but use the layby near to the Cat and Fiddle, not the pub car park as the present landlord, understandably does not take kindly to having his car park filled with non-drinking ramblers.

Head downhill along the road and take the first footpath on your right at a bend in the road (1). Very soon, fork right onto a clear track (2) signposted to Errwood. As the path heads downhill, be sure to take the path to Errwood Car Park, not to Errwood Hall (3). Beyond this point, as you pass a small wood on your right, the path bends to the right, away from the wall, towards the reservoir.

At the foot of the hill, turn right by a wall, then left to arrive at the road alongside the reservoir.

Turn left here and walk to the North end of the reservoir; follow the road across the dam (4), then begin to climb steeply. Just after a small pool (5) and a small plantation, turn left along a track alongside a wall. The track leads gently away from the wall and continues until just before a steep drop, near to a small rocky outcrop (6). Turn right here and continue uphill, passing through a gateway and, eventually, reaching a road (7).

Turn right here, then left just after a pool on your left, along the track of the old railway line, which is now an excellent wheelchair route. Walk along the track until just before the bricked-up tunnel entrance (8), where you turn left: there is a waymark and you simply follow the wall.

As the wall bends to the left, you fork right (9), again there is (or was) a waymark. Now go straight ahead to a stile to the right of a wood. Cross the stile and follow the path downhill – noticing Buxton ahead of you.

Where the footpath meets the road, turn right (10) and walk as far as the small lodge (11), when you turn right along the road past Plex Farm. At the end of this road, turn left (12) to re-join the old railway.

At the end of the line, we bear right to join the old Buxton-Macclesfield road, now little more than a track. After about 100 yards, turn right through a stile (13) signposted "Shining Tor and Lamaload". Walk uphill, following the wall on your right. At the first right hand corner in the wall, the path continues uphill but now moves away from the wall – the first part is well worn and should start you off in the right direction.

As the path reaches the top of the first hill (i.e. the one you are climbing), you should see a stile to the left of a group of trees (14). If you need a further indication it is in the top left corner of the area of moorland you are walking, at the junction of two walls. Cross the stile and continue in roughly the same direction along a well used path, all the way down to the River Goyt. It is worth completing the whole walk just to enjoy this stroll through gently changing, but always attractive moorland.

Cross the bridge over the Goyt (15) and walk up towards the road, where you turn right. Follow the road until you reach a track leading to the left (16), just before an old quarry. The track is waymarked and leads uphill, to the left of a picnic site.

Turn right at the first stile you reach and walk through the forest, eventually leading to a bridge over a stream (17). Cross this, and again follow the path into the forest. You emerge from the forest via a stile and continue straight ahead with a wall on your left and the forest on your right.

Eventually your path crosses a track – keep going, with the fence on your right as you commence a rather strenuous uphill slog. Keep alongside the fence, then the wall, all the way to the top, to where the path meets a track (18).

This is, of course, almost where you started, but it is worth pausing here for a moment or two as the view facing you can be quite magnificent, and you might well not have noticed it when you set out on on the walk. You'd be hard put to have more impressive weather conditions than the last time I was here. It was about half past six on a crisp March evening. There had been an unseasonal fall of snow, which lay a few inches deep. Opposite, to the right of Shutlingsloe, the sun was a big red ball, just about to dip behind the hills – a perfect end to a beautiful walk.

I hope that you enjoyed this walk as much as I did. Now, turn left and follow the track back to the road and your car.

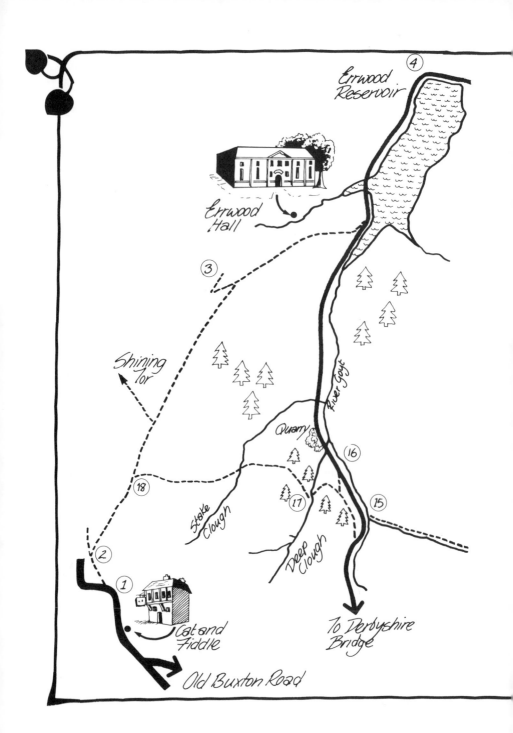

Errwood Reservoir

④

Errwood Hall

③

Shining Tor

River Goyt

Quarry

⑯

Stake Clough

⑱

⑰

Deep Clough

⑮

②

①

Cat and Fiddle

To Derbyshire Bridge

Old Buxton Road

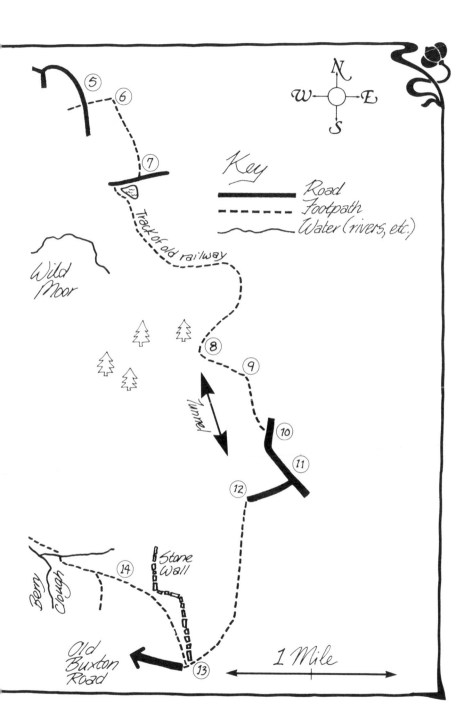

Wilmslow

This section is the largest in the book, in terms of the total number of walks. Partly, this is due to it being my "local patch", but also because it includes parts of Styal, Chorley, Great Warfield and Mobberley. The walks themselves all begin in Wilmslow, before straying over the boundaries.

Wilmslow, like Alderley Edge, is very much a railway town in that the railway companies offered incentives to house builders in the shape of cut-price tickets to Manchester. Because of this, there are those who argue that Wilmslow has no history but, just to prove them wrong, there is the little matter of "Lindow Man" or whatever is his currently popular name. This well-preserved body was discovered in the peat deposits of Lindow Common – an area of parkland that just about deserves the title of "beauty spot"; fortunately, some improvements are in hand which may well have smartened Lindow up by the time you read this book.

The peat of Lindow has been a small local industry for many years. Some peat is still cut but, in a 1935 edition of Cheshire Life, it was reported that thousands of pieces of peat were cut every day. The work must have been hard, for each worker alone was said to cut around 1000 pieces per day – indicating that the workforce must have been fairly small. Most of the peat was used for firelighters, after being soaked in creosote.

The name "Wilmslow" derives from the Anglo-Saxon for "William's Mound" and then, as now, the surrounding land must have been primarily agricultural. In between times, there have been other industries, notably the silk and cotton mills dotted around the area. Wilmslow's own silk mill was operational until 1923, when it was burnt down, due, it was thought, to the unsafe storage of gelatine. Of far greater importance was, and is, Quarry Bank Mill at Styal which was developed in various stages by the Greg family from 1787 to 1939, when it was handed over to the National Trust. The mill lies at the centre of Styal Country Park and is of interest not only as a restored cotton mill, but also as the hub of a self-contained village. You can still see the mill workers' houses and visit the chapel, school and apprentice house.

The mill lies on the River Bollin which, despite local folk-lore, has no provable connection with Anne Boleyn. The Bollin is very influential on the area both in terms of motive power for the old mills, and for its effect on the landscape as it meanders along the wide area of the Bollin Valley.

The Walks

As I have indicated, this is rich agricultural land. The walks are all "easy" but varied, both in their connections with local history, and the variations in terrain. The land is gently undulating, being at its best around the Bollin.

The old weir on the Bollin

To look at the map, you might think that this area is flat (which, in the main, it is) and boring (which it certainly is not). Something which you will not see on the Ordnance Survey Map are the paths shown in my map (below). This is because many of the paths alongside the Bollin are permissive ones, meaning that the landowner (in this case, the National Trust) is allowing walkers on the paths but that they are not definitive in the O.S. sense. These paths are a superb bonus, as you'll see.

The walk begins at Twinnies Bridge (1) which is near to a car park at the west end of The Carrs recreation ground. You enter the car park from Styal Road (see map). Alternatively, begin at the Wilmslow Parish Hall end of The Carrs which enables you to take either the obvious "dog-walker's" route alongside the Bollin, or the less obvious path through the wooded slope on your extreme left as you walk through The Carrs. This is rather more rewarding, as it takes you past the now-ruined private chapel which belonged to Pownall Hall. This path drops down to Pownall Bridge, previously the main route to Pownall Hall, and then to the car park, where the main party are waiting for us!

From here, simply follow the popular path (2) to Styal Mill. If this is already too familiar, try the Worm's Hill route for a change. The lower path is part of the "Apprentices' Walk" so called because the Styal Mill apprentices, under the watchful eye of their boss, Samuel Greg, walked along here – and then to Wilmslow Parish Church – for spiritual uplifting.

Styal Mill, "Museum of the Year" for 1984, is certainly worth a visit – or perhaps many visits as it is constantly changing. One of its particular charms is that it is a working mill, in Cheshire countryside albeit on a small scale compared to its former glory. A major attraction is the water wheel, which has restored the Mill to its 19th Century splendour.

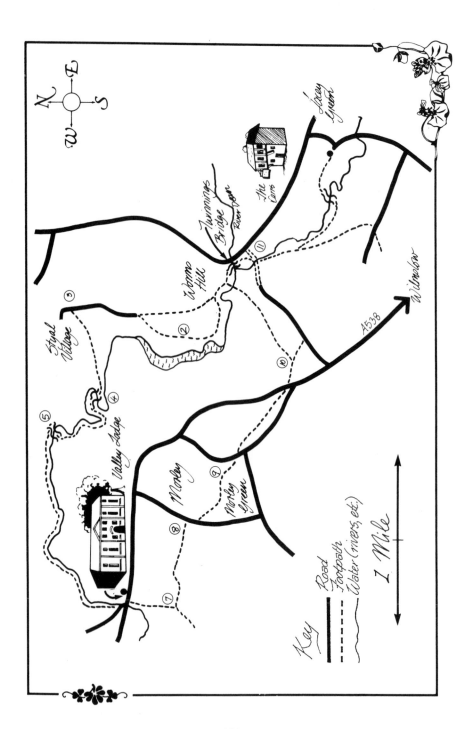

Carry on past the mill, up the tarmac drive and past Quarry Bank House. Note the footpath to Morley on your left, the old packhorse route from Northwich to Yorkshire. It was used to transport salt from Cheshire to Yorkshire and wool on the return journey. An added advantage was the fact that it avoided crossing the Lancashire boundary and, therefore, escaped two sets of tolls. As you walk up the drive, you might also notice the occasional large-ish cobblestone set into the left-hand side of the drive: these enabled the horse drawn carts to rest for a moment, by backing their wheels on to them.

But, enough of history; a hundred yards or so up the drive, turn sharp left along the footpath into the Northern woods above Quarry Bank House. Walk straight through these very attractive woods, avoiding side-turns, until you reach the Bollin again, which you follow downstream to a flat area. Nearly at the farthest reach of a wide sweep of the river, you will find a bridge (4), which you cross and then turn left. The bridge is called a "helicopter bridge" because, would you believe, that's how it was dropped into place!

Now follow the path to "Giant's Castle" alongside a crazily-meandering Bollin that will often convince you that you are going the wrong way – you're not – so long as you reach the next "new" bridge (5). This is of interest because it was largely paid for by the proceeds of a sponsored walk from Land's End to John 'O' Groats.

Cross the bridge and follow the path to Oversley Ford, emerging on the "old" road by the Valley Lodge Hotel (6). From here – perhaps pausing for a refreshment stop if you've timed it right – cross the A538 and cross the crash barrier immediately to the left of the bridge. At the time I last walked this path, teams of workers were busily installing stiles and steps (for the infirm?) – I felt a bit cheated, really! The path goes initially by the river, up a steep slope and straight across a large field (it used to run along a hedge, but that's disappeared in the name of progress). Then, over a smart new bridge (7) at which you turn left (signposted "Morley Green" towards Shady Grove (8).

At the road, turn right and, after fifty yards or so, left at the "Nans Moss Lane" sign. Follow the hedge into the second field and head toward Moss Grove Farm (9). Cross the minor road and continue along the path opposite the farm towards Mobberley Road. Walk along this road, to the A538; cross over to a path and turn left at the first pair of stiles (10). Follow a pleasant path through the woods, behind King's Road and Wilmslow Rugby Club to re-join the Bollin. Very soon, you'll see a bridge (11) which you cross – and you're just about back to the car park.

This must be the pleasantest walk in the Wilmslow area – and it is interesting to reflect that it is only possible because of that sponsored walk – otherwise you'd have to swim across the Bollin!

Note: the term "Apprentices' Walk" was coined by Wilmslow Historical Society just a few years ago – it does not date back to Greg's time!

Walk: W2

Starting Point: Wilmslow Parish Church or George and Dragon. (SJ848815)

Route: Wilmslow to Mottram Bridge.

Length: Five miles, easy.

Duration: Two hours, approximately.

Although this is an "easy" walk, it is not without its problems. I suggest that you walk through two cultivated fields, along what are believed, at the time of writing, to be public rights of way. Eventually, there may be an official diversion, but not yet!

A convenient starting point is Wilmslow Parish Church car park at the entrance to the Carrs or the George and Dragon, depending on the hour of day and what kind of uplifting you need. Walk along Mill Street, cross Manchester Road to Bollin Walk. At the end of this road, take the footpath under the railway arches (1) to Bollin Bridge (2), where you turn right towards Macclesfield Road. Cross the road, and almost opposite is a tarmac path to Thorngrove School (3). This is where the "real" walk begins.

The path enters a field and bends to the left, following a hedge. After 50 yards or so, you come to the corner of a large field – actually several fields ploughed into one, so the old field boundaries are almost obliterated. According to the map, the path crosses the field diagonally, joining a hedge on the far side. The hedge is kept on one's right; you then cut across a triangle of land, ending up at a stile. This is all very well in the winter time, but when the farmer has grown a knee-high crop here, you may have problems. So, you might like to chicken out and walk around the right hand edge of the field, again arriving at the same stile. Cross this, and another, and go through a wood to Hough Lane (4).

Turn right and walk along Hough Lane to Chonar Farmhouse (5), where a footpath runs between the first and second buildings, over a stile, through a small field to a gate. From here, go straight ahead to join a row of trees (the remains of an old hedge), and cross the stile where the line of trees meets a hedge.

146

Turn left, and follow the hedge which again breaks up into isolated trees, carrying on to a large hole (6), filled with debris. Here comes the second problem! The same farmer who cultivates this land has also removed certain hedgerows. So, from this hole in the ground, you have to navigate your way across another ploughed field, heading for a large tree roughly in the middle of the hedge facing you across the field. You should find yourself crossing the drive to "Oak Hollow" (previously Hole Farm) and you should be facing a well-maintained stile (7).

Cross this stile, into grounds belonging to Oak Hollow, and follow the planked fence to another stile. You cross the stile and find yet another problem – you guessed it – the field boundaries have again been removed in the interests of prairie farming. But, carry on: cross the field, keeping a wooded pool on your right, then towards another wooded pool which you keep on your left. The path then bends to the left and heads for the Prestbury road through a narrow gap to the right of a tall conifer hedge. On emerging from this path onto the main road, there is a sign (8):

"Thomas Lockerby Footpath Fund.
To Hough Green and Alderley Edge"

Thomas must be turning in his grave!

From here onwards, it really is easy. Turn right and walk for just over a quarter of a mile along the main road, then turn left (9) at the impressively poplar-lined drive to Dean Farm. (alternatively, turn right along the farm drive just after the Wilmslow sign, before our suggested left turn, which leads up to Alderley Edge: consult a map – it is a little-used path.)

Presuming you are still with me, go through Dean Farm and follow the yellow waymark signs (in reverse) alongside a large fence to Mill Lane. Here, turn left, cross Mottram bridge, and turn left to head home to Wilmslow. It really is so easy from here – nice yellow arrows, footpath signs, the lot: just like the first part of the walk ought to have been.

There's not a lot to say about this easy section of the walk. But do look out for the weir (12) in the Bollin, which was used to control the water level to the mill. Look carefully on your left and you'll find the old mill race below the houses in Macclesfield Road.

For a longer walk, you have the choice of walking from Mottram Bridge to Mottram St. Andrew or Prestbury, on either side of the Bollin. The paths are beautifully waymarked and a credit to the Bollin Valley Project.

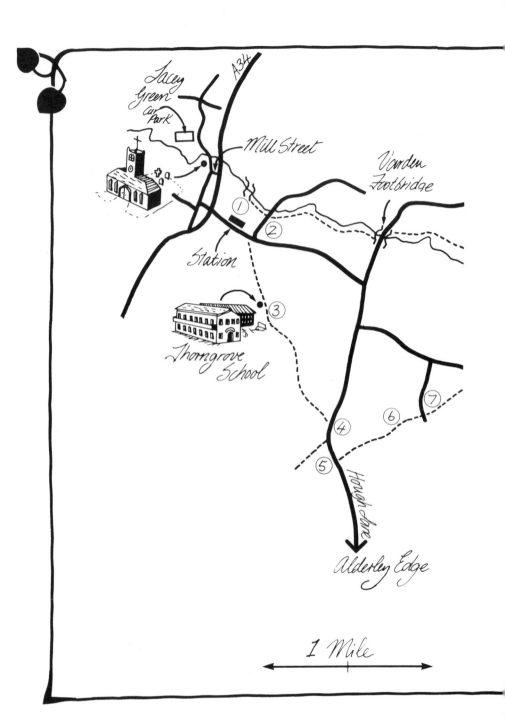

Lacey Green Car Park

A34

Mill Street

Vardem Footbridge

Station

① ② ③ ④ ⑤ ⑥ ⑦

Thorngrove School

Hough Lane

Alderley Edge

1 Mile

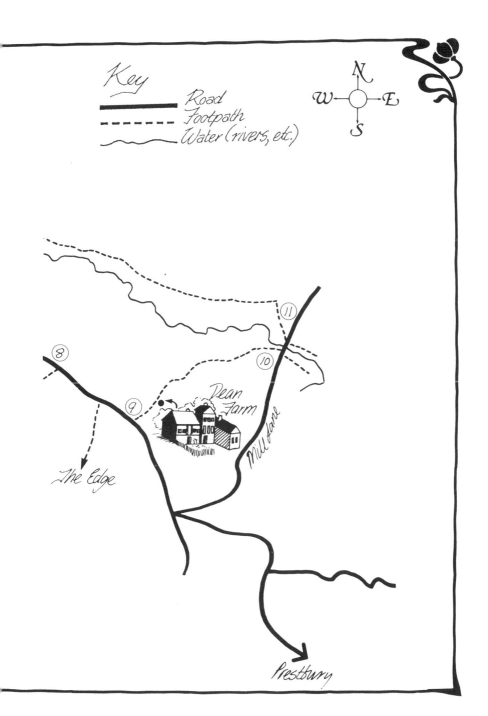

Walk: W3

Starting Point: Car park in Racecourse Road (SJ833814)

Route: Wilmslow to Castle Hill

Length: Seven and a half miles. Easy.

Duration: Three hours

Parents will easily be able to persuade their children to come on this walk – so long as they are interested in aeroplanes. For, not only does it cover a lot of very typical Cheshire countryside, it also goes past the end of the main runway!

Start by parking at the car park in Racecourse Road, off the A538 near the Boddington Arms (1). Walk back to the A538 and, in the Altrincham direction past the petrol station to a left turn. Soon, take the path (2) marked Nan's Moss Lane. Walk along this path, taking a stile to the right of a farm (3). Head slightly to the right and follow the path, with the hedge on your right, emerging through a narrow corridor of hedges to Morley Green Road (4).

Turn right and walk along this road to the drive to "Shadygrove". Turn left here and walk down the drive, over the stile and through a generally muddy section across a waymarked field, heading towards the far corner of the field, and across a small bridge alongside the Bollin. Note that you can connect up with walk W2 just before this point (5).

Follow the path (very muddy in winter) above the Bollin to a sloping field below Bollin House farm. The path leads up the hill to a farm drive (6), where you can cut the walk short (and miss the planes!) by turning left towards Oak Farm and Burleyhurst Lane.

The path does not follow the drive all the way to the farm. Instead, just before the drive bends to the right, the footpath shoots off to the left, behind the hedge on your left. Follow the path behind Beehive Farm. Note that the stiles at (7) are staggered – cross over the first and the second one is a little to your right.

The path continues to the left of the next farm as far as a well made service road (8) preceded by a stile. Facing you, over the road, is a stockaded "ILS" area for the airport. Cross the road to a stile, then work your way around the ILS area, keeping it on your left. After two stiles, you come to a third stile which heads right: you will see a stile in the hedge about mid-way along. This path leads you to the drive to Castle Hill farm. (It also led me to a "Beware of the Bull" sign at the end of this public footpath – was this an invitation for me to trespass, so as to avoid the bull? – farmers take note!)

Just a few yards along the farm drive is a stile to the left. Hop over this, go to another stile virtually opposite and through another field, keeping a wooded pool on your right. The next stile is in the left hand corner of the field. Go over this and head for yet another stile midway along the hedge adjacent to a large tree and a small pool. (This time obstructed by an electric fence – a lot of fun, these walks!) The path then bends to the left, passing to the left of two pools to another stile (11). There are about 30 stiles on this walk!

Now cross a smaller field than the previous one and head for the top left hand corner, where there is a gate (12). Turn left here, and go through a series of gates and old stiles, past Stock in Hey Farm (13), where there is an abomination of a stile just after crossing the farm drive.

Keep walking in a straight line to the staggered (left/right) junction over Woodend Lane (14), from where you head towards Oak Farm (15), which is the leftmost of the two groups of buildings visible. The footpath goes through the fields (often cultivated or ploughed) to a footpath sign just to the right of the farm. Use the centremost electricity pylon as a sight line to guide you approximately to the footpath sign.

Turn left here and take the path immediately to the right of the farm. This path passes to the right of the farm buildings and through a series of stiles towards Burleyhurst Lane. After a few hundred yards or so (about half way to Burleyhurst Lane) the path gives you the choice of walking to the left or right of the hedge; the map indicates that you keep to the right of the hedge, whilst most walkers keep to the left.

Turn left at the road and walk to Burleyhurst Farm. Almost opposite to this is an entrance (16) with a footpath sign leading into a tree nursery.

Proceed straight ahead until you pass a sign pointing to the right (17). Ahead of you is an old stile leading to a lake. Turn left and head across the field towards a stile adjacent to a gate. The following instructions are freely adapted from those at the end of walk W5.

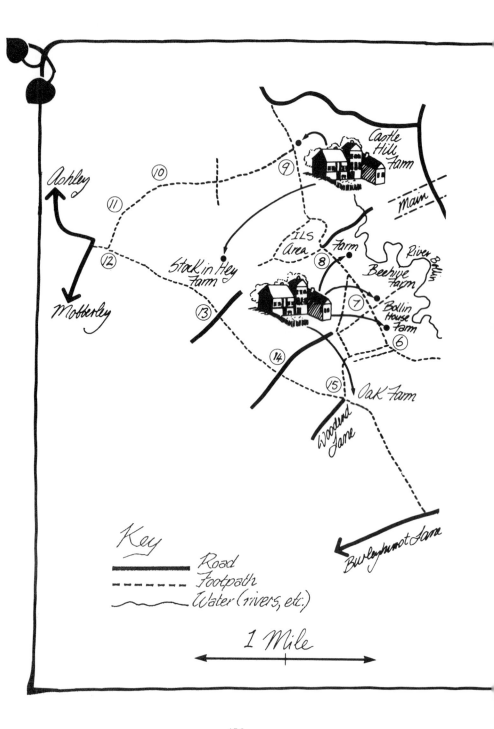

Ashley

Mobberley

Castle Hill Farm

Main

ILS Area

Farm

River Bollin

Beehive Farm

Stock in Hey Farm

Bollin House Farm

Oak Farm

Woodend Lane

Burleyhurst Lane

⑩ ⑪ ⑫ ⑬ ⑭ ⑮ ⑨ ⑧ ⑦ ⑥

Key

Road
Footpath
Water (rivers, etc.)

1 Mile

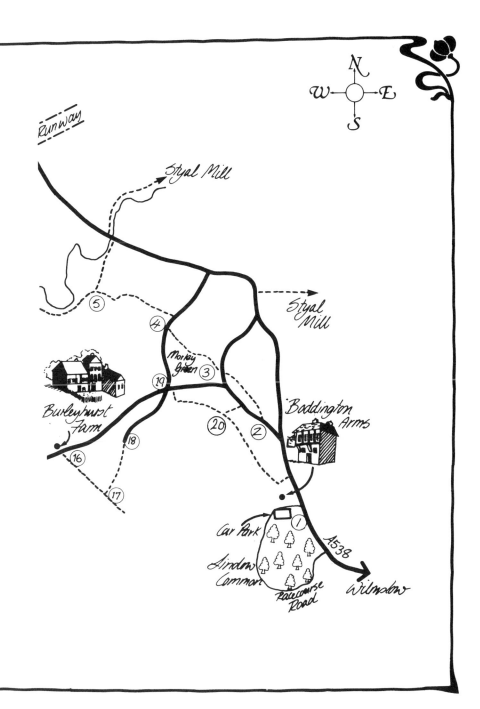

Runway

Styal Mill

Styal Mill

⑤

④

Morley Green

③

⑲

Burleyhurst Farm

⑳

②

Boddington Arms

⑱

⑯

⑰

Car Park

①

Lindow Common

Racecourse Road

A538

Wilmslow

N
W • E
S

The path leads over a small hill to a stile in the top right hand corner of the field (18). Go through this and then along Eccups Lane to Mobberley Road (19).

Turn right, then right again along a track opposite to Morley Green Road. Turn left at the first house you come to and continue along a wide path. Where it bends to the left, go through a gate on your right (20) and go straight ahead with the hedge on your right until you reach Greaves Road. Follow this to Altrincham Road, turn right and return to the car park.

Those of a nervous disposition may care to read my cautionary warning about bulls at the end of walk W5.

Towards Bollin House Farm, from the Bollin Valley.

The Plough and Flail is at the end of Paddock Hill Lane which, in turn, is mid-way between North Cheshire Garages (near to Brook Lane, Wilmslow) and the Bird in Hand pub at Knolls Green. Paddock Hill Lane is opposite to the road leading to Wilmslow Golf Club, if a further clue is needed. Presuming that you have now found the right spot, doubtless the publican would be happy to have you use the car park in anticipation of slaking your thirst on your return – but ask him first or park nearby if you'd rather not bother.

From the Plough and Flail turn left and walk along the road to a drive on the right (1). The path goes to the left of the drive, unmarked except by a stile. Go down a narrow, often overgrown passage, over a stile and through the next field to a collection of buildings (2). Pass in front of the buildings, over a drive and through the gate.

The path then bends to the right and through the middle of a wooded area to a stile (of sorts). Scramble over this and join the path through the trees, opposite. This becomes a clear path, after 100 yards or so, with trees either side. The paths around here all are based on peat (Lindow was once a prime peat producing area) and hence are inclined to be very soggy. Those of you with an interest in history may like to follow up the research into findings about "Lindow Pete" (get it?) – a body several thousands of years old excavated in Lindow in 1984, in remarkable condition. The path eventually becomes a minor road and emerges at a main road (3).

Turn right here, cross the road, and turn left down Carr Lane. Go down the lane, past the sewage works, then down the drive to Carr Bank Farm (another path goes to the right from here, just by the farm gate). Your path leaves the farm drive by way of a stile into a field in front of the farm. Keep to the left and cross the "stile" at the end of the field, then head to the right, through some farm buildings and in front of a house, to a farm drive.

155

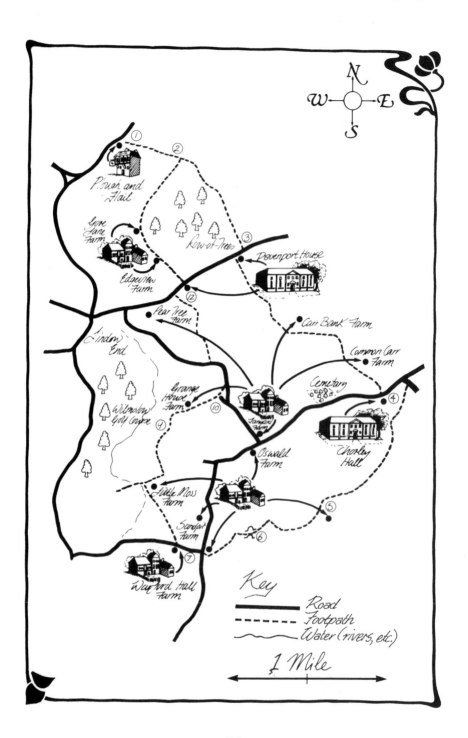

Key

Road
Footpath
Water (rivers, etc.)

1 Mile

Eventually, the path goes to the right, and the fence goes to the left. You turn left here, towards a white house on the main road. Follow the fence, then a stream, to the road (4).

You are now on the outskirts of Alderley Edge. Turn left and take the first turn right, along Chorley Hall Lane, getting glimpses of Chorley Old Hall as you go.

Now turn right along an unsigned track, opposite Windermere Drive. Follow the track to a minor road, keep right, then almost immediately join another track, a well made one this time. At the private drive to Field's Farm, the footpath heads straight on, behind a conifer hedge, then behind several large greenhouses (5). Just keep the hawthorn hedge on your right and carry straight on.

Cross the first stile that you come to and then, after a few yards, you meet a fence with a stile set in it. Do *not* cross this stile; instead, turn left and follow the fence on your right all around the edge of the field. This path crosses a stile, passes under the electricity cables and comes to yet another stile.

Turn left here and head for a footbridge (6) over a small stream. After crossing this, bear slightly to the right, towards a gate. Go through this and head for the farm buildings. The path enters the farmyard by a gate and goes immediately in front of the farmhouse, then turns right to the road. (As an aside, the farmer here would have, in my opinion, a very good case to apply for a diversion in order to protect his privacy. Failing this, a good alternative might be for him to waymark a concessionary path which most reasonable people would use.)

Cross the road to Merryman's Lane and, after one hundred yards or so, turn right at the footpath sign (7) just before a house. The path runs alongside a hedge and carries straight on, over two stiles. After the second stile, walk alongside the hedge of a "prairie" field to a large single oak tree. Turn right here and head towards Little Moss Farm (8). Turn left at the next fence, down a track which follows the fence over a stream in the right hand corner of the field to a stile. Cross over this to another prairie.

Walk along the right hand edge of this field, past a pool. From here, the path correctly goes straight across the field to Grange House Farm, though you may wish to chicken out and walk around the edge. The path goes past Grange House Farm (10) and Willow Tree Farm in quick succession, along a track. Immediately after Willow Tree Farm, the track bends to the right and there is a stile on the left. Hop over this to the next stile, where you continue past Orrells Well Farm (11) along the road. (Do not cross the road to the footpath sign here.)

The path enters a field where the road passes below the electricity cables. Head across the field to the left hand side of the hedge facing you. (This field is ploughed and cultivated, but you are within your rights.) When you reach this hedge, follow it around to a stile roughly where the hedge turns right. Now just follow the stiles to the main road.

Turn right here, then left along Gore Lane (12). At the end of the lane, there is a stile in the hedge between two houses. Cross this, then three more stiles, taking you back to location (2), the collection of buildings. Turn left here, and you're back at the Plough and Flail!

Lindow Moss, Wilmslow (photo: Rosalind Bramley)

Walk: W5

Starting point: Car park in Racecourse Road.

Route: Lindow, Saltersley and Mobberley. (SJ833814)

Length: Nine and a half miles, easy.

Duration: Four hours, approximately.

This is an "easy" but admittedly lengthy walk, for our Wilmslow group. Although it goes along some familiar routes, some little-used footpaths are included, which I feel are important in our local path network – especially when you need to plan circular walks like this one. Note: many paths cross this area and you will definitely need a 1:25000 OS map – be warned!

This walk begins at the car park in Racecourse Road, opposite the Boddington Arms. Follow Racecourse Road to Lindow Lane (2), otherwise cross Lindow Common if you know the paths. Go down the lane to the Bridleway (signed), along the drive to the first house on the left (Bramford).

The path continues past Bramford, then turns right, through a wooded area, eventually joining another path, at a T-junction (3). Turn right here. After about 100 yards, turn left (4) along a wide track; keep straight ahead when, after a few hundred yards, a path joins from the left. The path now becomes increasingly peaty – and squelchy in the winter – so wellingtons are recommended. Turn right at the next T-junction (5) (if you turn left, this takes you to "Stormy Point", at the end of Moor Lane, which is an alternative way to start or finish – prematurely – our walk).

This path now takes you past the old peat workings – see if you can find the remains of a narrow gauge railway used to transport the peat!

When you reach the crossroads(6), you are at the westerly end of Newgate. Turn left here, passing a bungalow on your right. The footpath goes to the left of a lake – the remains of a flooded sandpit. (A second path originally went straight ahead here, being diverted to the right as the sandpit grew in size. The stile at the north-westerly end is still there, but at the Newgate end, you are welcomed with barbed wire. It's now two years since I took up the cudgels to have the path diverted along the north shore of the lake – the wheels of local government grind slowly!)

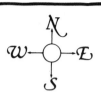

Key

Road
Footpath
Water (rivers, etc.)

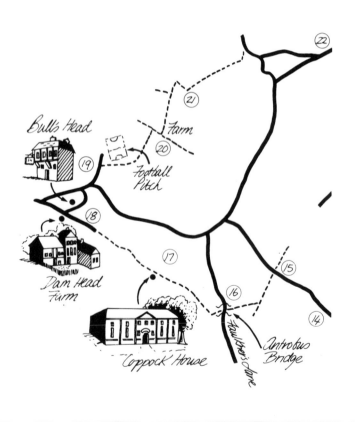

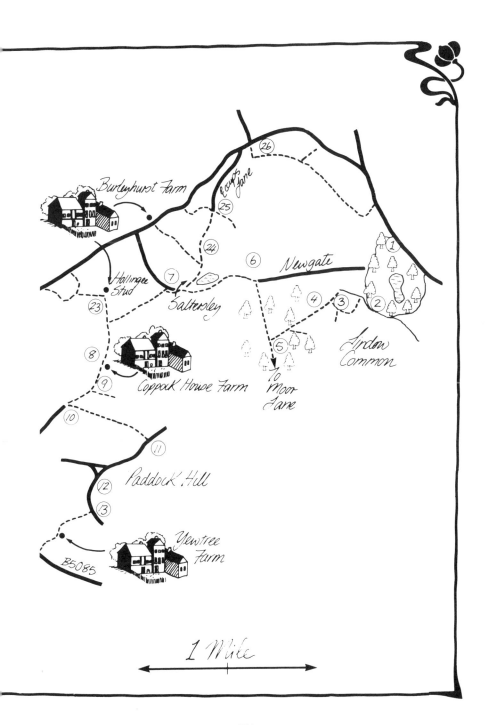

Burleyhurst Farm

Hollinger Stud

Saltersley

Coppock House Farm

Newgate

Lindow Common

To Moor Lane

Paddock Hill

Yewtree Farm

B5085

1 Mile

Carry on past Saltersley Hall Farm (on your right), joining the farm drive. Turn left at the stile (7) after about 100 yards, and cross the field to a stile adjacent to a gate roughly half-way along the hedge that is facing you.

From here, the path goes straight ahead with the hedge on your left for the first few yards. Continue, with the hedge to your left and head to the large single oak tree, and then straight ahead to the middle of the wooded area.

At the fence, you should find yourself looking at the back of "Hollingee". The wooden fence forms a dog's leg with an older fence and the path goes over the remains of a stile (jealously guarded by a fake electric fence on my last visit. Perhaps somebody might pinch the stile?). Go to the left of the leftmost of a pair of oak trees, and up a slight slope. (Do not go into the flat field on your right.) Go over this small hump to the hedge, where you turn left to Coppock House Farm (8). The path goes through the farm to join the farm drive.

About fifty yards past the end of the drive, there is an old stile (9) which will take you back to the Plough and Flail if you wish to shorten the walk. Otherwise, carry on past a group of houses.

Before you reach the garage (Renault body repair) turn left down a drive (10) to the right of a modern house, over a barely-recognisable stile adjacent to a farm gate. The path goes through a small field to a second gate. From here, go straight through the next field, under the electricity cables, to a stile.

The path now runs alongside the hedge over a stile (of sorts) towards the road, where you turn right (11).

This quiet country lane passes through Paddock Hill. Continue for about half a mile, then fork left down Paddock Hill Lane (12).

After about a quarter of a mile, at the end of a Z-bend, there is a bungalow called "White Croft" on your left. The path goes through the gate on your right and runs alongside the hedge to Yew Tree Farm. The path goes through the farm and along the drive to join the main road to Knutsford (14). The observant should note that there is a second path from just after the bend in the farm drive to the main road – the footpath sign is clearly visible, but there is no stile at the farm end and the field is always ploughed up or cultivated. Naturally, it is your right to walk it if you wish; perhaps a quiet word in somebody's ear?).

Turn right along the main road, passing that signpost and noticing the absence of a stile. Walk along the road for about half a mile, and turn left just before Sunny Bank Farm (15), a small half-timbered black and white building. The path, though unsignposted, is clearly visible and runs between two hedges to a stile.

Cross the stile, and go through the next field to another stile. From here, head to the top right hand corner of the field to yet another stile. Cross this, and continue to the road (16). Turn left here, go over the bridge, then turn right up a drive. At the first house, Brown Owl Cottage, go into its drive and cross the stile just a few yards past the gate. The next stile is facing you at the opposite side of the field. The path continues alongside the hedge of the next field and then, at the end of the hedge on your left there is a stile; cross this and continue in the same direction that you were walking, towards Coppock House, nestling in the woodland. To find the next stile, follow the fence to the corner of the field; turn left, then after fifty yards, you'll see a stile and a footbridge. Pass behind Coppock House (17) to a gate at the corner of the building. Go through this, turn left, and the next stile is facing you, after going a few yards along the drive.

Continue straight along the path, crossing over to the left of the field boundary at the end of a hedge, eventually reaching a stile in the corner of a field. From here, cross the field by heading slightly to the right, towards a wooded area (or walk round the edge to be kind to the farmer). The stile is adjacent to the gate; cross this and carry on past Dam Head Farm (18), to the road, where you turn right and pass (or stop at) The Bull's Head on your left – also the Roebuck, a little further back. (Interestingly, "Dam Head Farm" is appropriately named: there was a lake, and a dam, but no longer).

Where this road joins the main road cross over to the tarmac footpath and turn right. At the next road, turn left along Church Lane. The footpath is now on the right, opposite to "Gorsey Brow"(19). Clamber over the derelict stile, or the gate to play safe. Cross this field diagonally, to the gate in the top right-hand corner. Cross the next field and again make for the gate near the top right-hand corner. From here, there is a maze of paths and, to make things worse, there are small discrepancies between the paths as shown on the map and as they exist on the ground – so you'll need to follow these directions very carefully:

Go through the gate and cross the small field facing you. Keep the hedge on your left and, just after the hedge bends away to the left, you will find a passing place – 'stile' is too generous a word – to the immediate right of a tree. Cross this and go straight ahead (due north) to the top corner of the next field, where you will find a stile between a tree stump and a holly hedge.

Continue in the same direction as far as the next hedge, where you cross a stile next to a gate and turn right. Walk on for a hundred yards or so, with the hedge on your right – the map incorrectly shows the path on the other side of the hedge. Turn left at the corner of this field and continue towards the end of the field, alongside the hedge, until you reach a gap in the hedge (21). Cross this, go through the nearby gateway, and continue in the same direction that you were previously walking, passing a single oak tree in the next field and then crossing a stile, of sorts, just to the right of a wood.

From here, head slightly to the right, passing a small depression on your left. The next stile can be found to the left of a row of oak trees, leading to a footbridge.

Passing through this field, I noticed the regular ridged pattern of the surface – each ridge being about 10–12' or so wide. Could this be a remnant of medieval ridge and furrow cultivation, or is it more recent?

Cross this and then go straight across the next field to a stile.
Turn right here, and walk along the road, turning left at the main road.

After 100 yards, turn right at the footpath sign (22), by the first gate you come to. Head towards the building (Hollingee) opposite to you, by walking to the right of the hedge, which is a little to your left. At the first large gap in the hedge, turn left, and cross the field to join the drive to Hollingee.

Just before the farm, there is a stile on your right (23). Cross this and walk alongside the fence, initially. After the fence turns to the left, continue in the same direction and cross the stile that is facing you.

From this point, turn left to head back to Saltersley Hall Farm. Since you have been here before, you should remember all of this, and it is virtually a straight line, but here are some points to note:

The next stile is sometimes tricky to find – it is tucked away in the top left hand corner of the field. Cross this, but continue in the same direction that you were walking. At the stile on the farm drive, turn right to Saltersley Hall Farm.

After passing the farm, turn left before the lake at a stile – now we're on to a different path than the one we used originally. Follow this path to the next stile, where you turn right. This path joins the path from Burleyhurst farm which used to continue through a stile on your right: no longer, due to the lake!

Cross directly over the next field to a stile adjacent to a gate (24). The following instructions are identical to those for map W3; only the numbers are changed! The path crosses a small hill, heading to the left. A house is visible from just after the stile. The next stile is in the top right hand corner of the field, where you turn left along Eccups Lane (25). Turn right at the end of Eccups Lane, then right along the track opposite to Morley Green Road (26).

Turn left at a house ("Sunnyside") and walk along the path. Where it bends to the left, go through the gate on your right and continue along the edge of the field, with the hedge on your right. (On two occasions, there has been an huge brute of a bull in this field so, take the Ramblers' Association's advice in this circumstance: trespass – go around the opposite edge of the field to avoid personal injury). The path eventually joins Greaves Road, then Altrincham Road. Turn right, and you've made it back home again!

Those of you who wish to avoid re-tracing your steps (the stretch from Hollingee to Saltersley) can instead walk from point (22) on the map to Burleyhurst Farm, then turn right along the unmarked path to join our route to point (24). This does, however, mean that you have to walk along a busy and somewhat dangerous road.

Black Lake, Lindow Common, before ...

... and after dredging and landscaping during 1987

Walk: W6

Starting point: Twinnies Bridge (SJ839823)

Route: Twinnies Bridge to Morley

Length: Three and a half miles, easy.

Duration: One and a quarter hours approximately.

This is a really easy walk that you can fit into a summer evening, with the children in tow.

The best starting point is the car park (1) at Twinnies Bridge on the Styal to Lacey Green Road. Alternatively, walk through The Carrs to Twinnies Bridge.

From here, walk to Styal Mill – either the popular route by the river, or over Worms Hill.

Just past the mill, watch out for a sign on your left, "To Morley" (2). Walk down the cobbled path – the old packhorse road for transporting salt to Yorkshire – and up to the farm; it's invariably rather muddy in the farmyard.

From here, walk to the main road (3), turn right, then left at the first road junction, towards Morley. After a quarter of a mile, turn left at the sign for Nan's Moss Lane (4). Follow the hedge into the second field and head to Moss Grove Farm (5). Continue towards Mobberley Road, then cross the A538 to the path (6) which leads behind the Pownall Park housing estate and Wilmslow Rugby Club, back to the car park.

For those of you who think that the previous paragraph is a bit short on detail – it's because we have been here before! See the last two paragraphs of Walk W1.

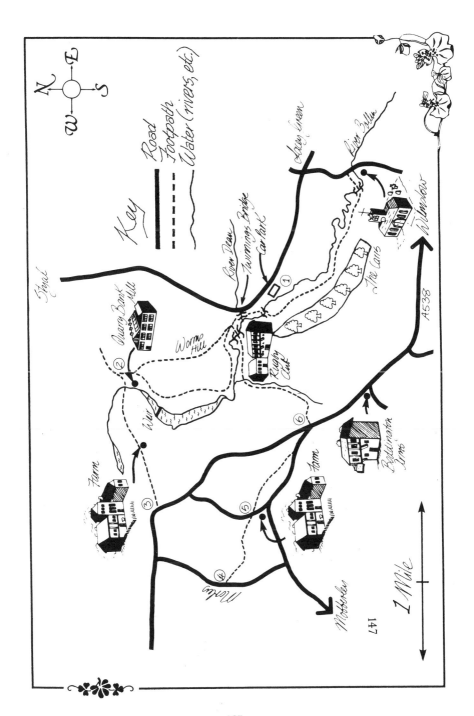

167

Styal Mill (by permission of the trustees).